LORD, TEACH US
TO PRAY

LORD, TEACH US TO PRAY

An intimate look into a maturing prayer life

MARY SHARON MOORE

AWAKENING VOCATIONS

Eugene, Oregon

To Brother Martin de Porres Gonzales
of Our Lady of Guadalupe Trappist Abbey,
who showed me early on what a soul
in love with God looks like.

CONTENTS

ACKNOWLEDGMENTS

I first was invited to speak on prayer on the spur of the moment. And I remember the moment well.

Back in the mid 2000s I was leading a group of Episcopal priests, along with their bishop, The Right Reverend Michael Smith, Bishop of North Dakota, in a Lenten retreat.

In my closing talk, Bishop Smith raised his hand, with the look of a question on his face.

Instinctively I did an interior check: Had I spoken some heresy? Or perhaps some theological foolishness?

"Can you speak to us of prayer," he asked.

Speak to us of prayer.

So I spoke of what I knew to be most true of prayer, and what I knew deeply in my own experience.

What I shared seemed to find a place, a resonance, in the hearts and minds of those present.

Sometime later I received a phone call, out of the blue, from Mike Benton, who worked in the offices of the Catholic Diocese of Boise, in Idaho. Although I had met him only once, many years earlier, he said that he had been following my work.

And he invited me to teach on prayer at the Fall Conference for the Diocese of Boise.

So again, I spoke of what I knew to be most true of prayer, and what I knew deeply in my own experience.

And again, what I shared seemed to find a place, a resonance, in the hearts and minds of those present.

More recently, a small group of pastoral-hearted laity surrounded me after a morning talk on prayer at Our Lady of Perpetual Help Church in Grove City, Ohio. Among them was Karen Cook, who invited me to return to their parish and offer an expanded version of the talk over the course of three evenings.

So I warmly thank Bishop Smith, Mike Benton, and Karen Cook for planting the seeds, for calling forth a harvest of thought from a maturing prayer life.

Wherever you are in your lives, may you walk in grace.

INTRODUCTION

Praying is like breathing, I often think. It simply is what we do, we of Christian faith.

Yet everyone breathes. So I like to think that, at some essential level, everyone also prays.

In fact, as I walk in my back yard beneath the canopy of big leaf maple and Ponderosa pine, beneath the predawn canopy of stars, raising my intercessions to God, I find all of creation breathing, praying, attending to the promise of a new day.

My apprenticeship in prayer began at age four. So what I share with you emerges from a lifetime of awakening to a living relationship with the Lord. Awakening to an invitation which is personal, unique, and given to everyone.

I was not aware that I had signed up for this apprenticeship. But apparently the student was ready, because the Teacher appeared.

The title, *Lord, Teach Us to Pray,* suggests a book on the Lord's Prayer. Many spiritual giants in the Christian tradition have written deeply and extensively on the Gospel accounts of Jesus' famous teaching. Saint Teresa of Avila and Saint John of the Cross come to mind.

And while we will explore the Lord's Prayer, I sense that I have much still to learn and precious little to add to the insights of these spiritual masters.

I am interested in exploring other lessons, other experiences, which the Lord offers in the school of prayer, lessons which draw forth and form and sustain the likes of you and me.

Each lesson, I notice, is customized to the student, and delivered when the student is ready for the learning. I discover that the student does not determine the season of readiness. The Lord does.

Nor does the student design the curriculum. The Lord does.

Yet what I discover is that the student must intentionally embrace the status of "student," and undergo the work of apprenticeship.

In short, showing up and being present to my life in its many assignments and challenges and invitations is perhaps the only way I can become this intentional student, the only way I can undergo discipleship on the way to being sent as an apostle of the Lord.

So I am speaking here of prayer that matures and readies us for actual apostleship—each of us, sent out, richly anointed, living our mission in the world.

I am speaking of prayer which bears actual fruit in the real world, in the circumstances which shape our lives and which touch the lives of others with grace and good.

I am not speaking of a program of study I might sign up for, but a way I am impelled to live my life, radically available to being shaped by the Master. Or, in the words of Saint Paul, embracing a way of life that seeks always to be "conformed to Christ."

My words about prayer cannot be a substitute for your prayer. There are no shortcuts to the one unique and intimate and honest conversation that means everything, and calls forth everything, and blesses everything in your life.

Over time you will notice patterns of prayer emerge, shaped by your life circumstances, colored by the lens of personality, and purified through disposition of heart and attitude and soul.

Your prayer forms, like mine, become a spiritual thumbprint—yours unique to you, mine unique to me. And through our prayer each of us shapes, in unique ways, the love and care and holy imagination which we bring to the world we touch in the course of our life.

In other words, prayer does not just happen. Any more than intentional and worthy and mature relationship with our closest others just happens. Prayer is the privileged conversation within the loveliest and most life-giving relationship you could ever imagine, a relationship that continually draws you forth, draws you beyond whom you have known yourself to be.

I might "choose" to pray in this way or that, and try out new techniques. But those deeper intimacies, those unself-conscious encounters with God, with the divine, choose me.

These holy encounters have been choosing me all along.

And you, no doubt, will begin to recognize the holy encounters that have been choosing you all along—whether you could name those encounters or not.

I am interested here in prayer which is a waking up, a maturing into anointed life in Christ, into life in Holy Trinity. I am vitally interested in waking up and maturing into a life which is a mission.

I am interested in prayer which is the flowering forth of your life and mine, in God, for the good of the world we touch.

Lord, Teach Us to Pray breaks into four sections. Part 1, "In the Beginning was the Word," explores prayer as "encounter."

Part 2, "The Intimate Conversation of Holy Trinity," considers prayer as "holy conversation."

Part 3, "Prayer as Invitation to Something More," is a self-paced retreat in three movements.

And in the Epilogue I share with you how I pray and, most important, why I pray.

Right now I pray that this book might serve as inspiration as you mature in the holy conversation of your own prayer life, and as you continue your journey into the Mystery who is God.

Mary Sharon Moore
January 1, 2017
Eugene, Oregon

PART 1

IN THE BEGINNING WAS THE WORD
Prayer as encounter

The sacred icon on the shelf beside my bed has intrigued me for years. For decades, really. It is called *Christ Pantocrator,* a sixth century icon from the Monastery of Saint Catherine, Sinai.

An opening reflection: Christ Pantocrator

You may know this sacred icon. It has a way of captivating the viewer. Once you see it, you cannot forget it.

When I contemplate this sacred icon, I see Jesus, preeminent Teacher, looking straight ahead, directly into me. But not quite. One eye meets mine straight on, delivering a gaze that originates in the place where wisdom and judgment meet, a gaze that demands from me an uncompromised accountability.

The other eye seems to gaze just beyond me, a softer gaze, compassionate. A gaze which is a cloak of sorts, to hide my shame. It is the eye of knowing, yes, and of deeply felt mercy.

I want to stay with the eye of softer gaze. Yet the eye of wisdom and judgment calls me back. The one, the other. The one essential to the other, if I am going to be honest as I stand before the Lord.

The truth of who I am in the Lord's eyes lies in their one penetrating gaze.

Now, I notice, the Master's right hand is raised in subtle gesture. Raised in benediction, perhaps. A quiet gesture, almost overlooked.

The index and middle fingers extend in duo, messaging his identity: the human and the divine dwelling together in this One, the Son of God.

His thumb and ring and small fingers touch, a small and quiet gesture which draws me to Holy Trinity.

Cradled in his left arm, secure against his chest, pressed close to the heart, is the book of the Gospels. The Word holding the Word. This treasure of words collected also reveals the Master's identity. Indeed, his mission.

Christ Pantocrator, Christ spanning all of creation, before and beyond all ages. "The Alpha and the Omega," I hear in Revelation, "the One who is and who was and who is to come, the Almighty" (see 1:8).

Of the many icons which fill my rooms, this is the one, with those all-knowing eyes, which watches over me as I sleep, which blesses me as I rise. The Word made flesh.

And only recently do I come to deeply understand that this right hand raised in blessing is blessing *me.* Not an image of a gesture of blessing, but an actual blessing, in this time and place. Ever new. I stand before the One who is, and who blesses me now. A blessing which falls upon my heart and mind and spirit like a commissioning, as fresh as this new day.

I let my gaze settle a while upon this hand raised in benediction: As though the hand had not been raised. And now it is, an eternally fresh gesture, divine benediction breaking into human time, into my time. Into this particular day, with its appointments and tasks, and its bothersome distractions.

The Christ of God, Lord of all creation, spanning before and beyond all time, encountering me, as I stand here now.

An opening Scripture: John 1:1-5, 14
"In the beginning was the Word"

I am drawn to the opening of Saint John's Gospel, drawn for reasons I cannot explain. I cannot easily get my arms around the high mystical language of this prologue, just as I cannot easily get my arms around the Mystery who is God.

Yet something knows something, I sense, when I read the words. Deep speaks to deep, as the Psalmist says (see Psalm 42:8).

"In the beginning was the Word," the Evangelist writes.

In the beginning of what, I wonder. And which word? There are so many.

These are the opening utterances of the holy elder John. He does not write of the beginning of something, or the beginning of anything, or even the beginning of everything. He writes of the beginning, before the "whatness" of things began to emanate from God.

"The Word was with God," John writes, "and the Word was God." Two, yet One.

John seems never to get over the wonder of this mystery, the mystery of indwelling, of abiding in, remaining in. These words weave like a golden thread through the fabric of his Gospel.

The Word now pours forth as Light, piercing a darkness which has not overcome it.

John does not write "a darkness which *did* not overcome it," as though there were a time when Light overcame the dark, but that was then, and the dark today just might elude the definitive piercings of Light.

No, he writes in the eternal present tense, a word of encouragement for us in our time, in our complex world: the Word, as Light, piercing a darkness which still has not overcome it.

A darkness which never will overcome the Light, no matter how tragic the realities of injustice and indifference, no matter the heart-wrenching stories of loss and suffering and death which remain untold behind the evening news.

Jesus himself went all the way down into death, down into the dark earth, his corpse sealed in the tomb. This is the darkness of which John writes. The Light seemingly snuffed out.

And then, resurrection happened. Irrepressible Light rising up triumphant over the forces of darkness and death. A shock of Light, no longer crucified Lord but risen Christ.

Now John gets to the part which I feel I can get my arms around: "And the Word became flesh," he writes, "and made his dwelling among us."

The Word of God, the Word which is God, has pitched his tent among us.

Word becoming flesh. Word pitching a tent. The images seem to not fit together.

Still, rejoicing swells my heart. I imagine his tent pitched among our tents. You know, that one tent which glows warmly, invitingly, from the inside.

Yet many of these tents, I notice, glow warmly, invitingly, from the inside.

Yes, these tents, all of them, where the holy light of welcome emanates, and the aromas of hospitality waft forth, and the embrace of community makes sure that no one is left standing out in the cold and dark.

To my amazement I discover that I have pitched my tent in the campsite of the Beloved Community.

The Word, become flesh, has pitched his tent among us, and we have seen his glory. And we are forever changed by what we have encountered.

A further reflection: I start with a word

To speak of prayer as encounter, I must enter first into the Word.

So I sit again with this mysterious phrase: The Word becomes flesh. The Word. God's self-expression.

And this divine self-expression becomes flesh, an actual distinct human being. One among us.

I sit a while with the words. I sit in the spaces between the words. These spaces, far from clustering into a dark void, I discover, are infused with Light.

The Word becomes flesh and … is entrusted to me.

The Word, entrusted to *me.*

I marvel at this revelation, even as the words form distinctly in my heart and in my imagination.

The Word becomes flesh, and is entrusted to me.

Instinctively I receive these words as they are: clear, strong, and missional.

What a sobering and deeply vital mission, I imagine, to enflesh in my own being this Word, to incorporate it, to carry it, to reveal it, to express it, to share it freely, to share it generously.

The Word, entrusted to me in every encounter.

The Word, entrusted to me for this time and place. Apart from what God gives to me, I have nothing to offer the world. And God gives the Word, entrusted now to me, so that I might make of it, again and again, my offering to the world.

I recall the beautiful words of twentieth-century Jewish philosopher Martin Buber: "You should utter words as though heaven were opened within them, and as though you did not put the word into your mouth, but as though you had entered the word."

I imagine the world's conversation, one day, consisting only of words uttered "as though heaven were opened within them." No other words allowed. Only words that open heaven. I want this world. I want to be a part of this beautiful and inviting conversation.

I am thinking now of the counsel of a friend: "Take care to speak in this place only what is most necessary, and in a quiet voice."

Do my conversations, I wonder, open heaven to those whom I encounter? Do I utter words as though I had entered the Word? This is my desire, surely. And to speak only what is most necessary, and in a quiet voice.

I desire to be led by the Holy Spirit in this ever-emerging relationship with the Word. I am willing to be surprised. In fact, I desire to be surprised.

The Word becomes flesh, and is entrusted to me. But when, exactly, does this enfleshment happen?

I think of my encounter, some time back, with Chuck, who is standing at the street corner with his cardboard sign in hand. A real zipper of a scar runs the length of his long, sad, slender face. I place myself right square in front of him. I pull out my earbuds and look into his eyes, into his face.

"How are you doing," I ask.

He tells me his story. We talk a while. I cannot explain it, but just like that, the Word becomes flesh. Together Chuck and I enter the Word. For a few minutes, at the northwest corner of Willamette Street and 29th Avenue, heaven is opened.

I think of my occasional encounters with Gonzalo, one of my "downtown people," who sits each day, sometimes alongside the library, sometimes at the transit mall, confined to his wheelchair. I am not too sure about his eyesight. And he is missing a leg.

"Gonzalo, es María," I say.

Maria is my street name.

"Cómo estás?" I ask him, suddenly realizing that I have just now used a good fifty percent of the words I know in Spanish.

He knows by now, and by my lousy pronunciation, that our conversation will be simple. He likewise stumbles as he tries out phrases in English.

But somewhere within these tortured attempts at words, attempts at conversation, the Word comes shining through.

"Gonzalo," I say, looking into his worn and beautiful face, "may I give you a hug?"

"Sí, María," he says.

The heavens open. A smile breaks across his face as his arms reach upward. He clings to me the way the child, feeling desperately alone, clings to the mother.

The Word becomes flesh, enfleshed, today, downtown, on the corner of Willamette Street and Broadway. Only for a moment or two. Enfleshed, nonetheless.

In encounters such as these, I learn how the Word becomes flesh. With each encounter I am apprenticed. I participate, in a small way, in the revelation.

Christ everywhere, and especially in the enfleshed encounter. Christ in the exchange of words, in the eyes looking into eyes, in the exchange of a sandwich and a bottle of water, passed from one hand to the other's outstretched hand. Christ in the blessing, Christ in the embrace.

A story: "In the beginning was … the ocean"

I am about four. Our family is vacationing overnight on the northern Oregon coast.

The ocean is new to me. This creaky wood-planked Victorian hotel with the high ceilings and tall rattling windows, and the clawfoot tub in the bathroom, with its black and white honeycomb tiled floor, all of this is new to me.

Sleeping in a bed not my own is new to me.

We watch the sun sink beyond the watery horizon. The rose glow of twilight gives way to a starry night sky.

"Daddy," I ask, as my father tucks me into my bed, "when does the ocean go to sleep?"

Perhaps this question reveals my four-year-old way of befriending the mighty Pacific, whose waves crest and crash, all shimmery in the silver moonlight, upon the shore beyond my window.

"Honey," my daddy says, "the ocean never sleeps."

In this instant—in this *instant*—I intuitively understand God. I receive the whole of the insight, as only a four-year-old can. Pure, and simple. In these few words I understand God.

Honey, the ocean never sleeps.

I have touched the lodestone.

Sleep comes quickly. I seem to intuit what I later will hear the Psalmist declare: "He collects the waves of the ocean; / he stores up the depths of the sea" (Psalm 33:7).

Perhaps, the four-year-old imagines, God's arms are in the starry heavens above me.

The budding contemplative

My young soul continues to grow in the natural way. And by age eight or so, I seem invited by the Lord to know him more intimately.

And being the only girl in the family, I fall into a particular role at home. After dinner, my mother becomes the dish washer. And I, by default, become the dish dryer.

Perhaps acting more out of need than out of craft, I find a way to, shall I say, escape my role as dish dryer, in order to tend to the invitation.

"Mother," I say, in a gentle and innocent way, "I need to go to the bathroom."

"Okay, dear," my mother replies. I feel secretly grateful that she does not question my timing.

I respectfully place my dish towel on the counter, and proceed down the hall to the bathroom. I have no recollection of whether I really need to go or not.

And after the appropriate amount of time, I come back up the hall. I tiptoe, a little dishonestly, no? And I find my way to the sofa in the living room.

In this moment, all I know is that my soul is completely composed, undisturbed by the sound of the dish washer sudsing and rinsing, and now drying the dinner dishes. I sit, fully composed in peace, with the Lord.

My stolen reverie is shaken by the not quite staccato sound of my mother's voice.

"Now where is that Mary Sharon," I hear her say.

I imagine her, from where I sit in the living room, with her hands on her hips. I truly think that she only now notices that I never returned from the bathroom. Perhaps she has been dreamy-eyed all this time, thinking about her day, her family, her life. I truly think she has no idea that I sit here, with my soul completely composed, on the sofa.

I know for certain, though, that I cannot explain to her my situation, the deep intuition that the Lord has invited me to sit with him, with the soul completely composed, on the sofa. I have no language for any of this. Only a felt understanding.

I cannot explain to her the beauty, the sheer serenity, the necessity, really, of this holy encounter.

Prayer as encounter

Prayer is many things. Your own experiences reveal as much. And chances are good that most descriptions of prayer in some way move us toward the heart of the matter.

I discover—and continue to be amazed at the discovery—that prayer, in its purest, most uncluttered and unadorned form, is an actual encounter.

Specifically, prayer is dynamic encounter with the Word. I return again to the prologue to the Gospel of John:

> In the beginning was the Word,
> and the Word was *with* God,
> and the Word *was* God.

These words draw me into a form of encounter which is immediate, intimate. Not merely an encounter of I-*and*-Thou, but an indwelling— that favorite word in John's Gospel—an enfleshed spiritual encounter of I-*in*-Thou.

In fact, in Jesus' final discourse in chapter 17 of John's Gospel, the language of dynamic encounter and enfleshed spiritual indwelling collapses upon itself, as Jesus prays to his Father "not only for [these whom you gave me] but also for those who will believe in me … so that they may all be one, as you, Father, are in me and I in you, that they also may be in us, … that they may be brought to perfection as one" (see John 17:20ff)

This prayer of Jesus could sound vaporous, were it not, in John's understanding, the prayer of the One who is the Word who is "with God" and who also "is God," and who has pitched his tent in a truly enfleshed way "among us."

Here Jesus not only speaks of prayer which is encounter. He himself, enfleshed Word who is "with God" and who "is God," is the prayer. To enter into prayer, then, is to enter into the Word who "is God" and who also "becomes flesh and makes his dwelling among us."

I am stretched as I ponder this mystery, that I am created for dynamic encounter with the Word.

So I should not be surprised that I am drawn to such encounter, an encounter that oftentimes I cannot get my arms around. An encounter which I cannot express in words, but which I can only intuit, and only when I am not trying hard to do so.

Being drawn to such encounter is never my initiative, I discover, but the initiative of the Spirit of the crucified Lord and risen Christ, hidden yet enfleshed within me. I cannot invite myself to such encounter. But I can respectfully knock at the door, and ask if an invitation might be waiting for me.

I know that I am created for dynamic encounter with the Word, because I am most myself when I engage in this encounter and then go outward and live accordingly.

The encounter is pure gift. The invitation to such encounter is pure gift. Even the longing, even the intuition that such encounter could await me, is pure gift.

A deeper look at "encounter"

I want to go to the heart of this word "encounter." What does it mean?

Encounter, quite simply, is a direct, open, unrehearsed meeting with another.

Encounter does not occur when I am merely thinking about you, or anticipating our meeting this afternoon over coffee. Encounter occurs when you finally arrive, and I look up from my magazine and see you standing beside my table, your face aglow with the delight of friendship and your arms extended, drawing me up for a joyful embrace.

Encounter is direct, immediate, in this enfleshed way. Encounter is a favorite word of Pope Francis, who shows us what a Gospel-driven enfleshed life looks like. It looks like a life of encounter, I encountering Thou.

In his inaugural exhortation *The Joy of the Gospel,* Pope Francis uses the word "encounter" thirty-two times. With a frequency like that, I know that I have to pay attention.

Francis writes of our "multifaceted culture of encounter," of special places of encounter, of adoration as prayerful encounter.

He writes, of course, of personal encounter with Jesus, of letting Jesus encounter us. He writes also of encountering the Lord's mercy, encountering the embrace and support of community, encountering beauty.

So encounter is direct engagement with another. It also is an open and unrehearsed meeting with another.

After we settle in with our coffees, you may tell me about your day, your week. And I might tell you about mine. Nothing new here, nothing surprising. We may know each other's narrative quite well. We may even be able to complete each other's sentences.

But when we move on to topics that matter, perhaps you tell me about an unexpected invitation you have received. Your eyes glow, your smile widens.

Or perhaps you tell me about an unexpected diagnosis you have received, and your eyes well up and your lip quivers.

The "open and unrehearsed" part of dynamic encounter with another is the unanticipated revelation of one self to another. What you reveal to me with your news, and what I reveal to you in my response, are the dynamics that make this encounter unique, sacred, and in a deep and mysterious sense, holy—revealing something of the mystery and holiness of God.

I encounter God at work in the circumstances of your life which itself is holy because your life flows from God who is holy.

When I deeply encounter another, when I deeply encounter you, I enter as though into an experience of prayer. Something true of you is revealed to me, and here something true of the divine is revealed to me through you, and through this dynamic encounter.

Jesus encounters his Father

The Gospels give us glimpses into Jesus' dynamic encounter with his Father, both in his prayer and in his encounters with others.

"Father," Jesus says, "what you have hidden from the clever ones in the world, you have revealed to mere children" (see Matthew 11:25; Luke 10:21). His observation is not unique, yet noticing this simple truth of humanity evokes in Jesus a spontaneous prayer of praise to his Father.

In John's account of the raising of Lazarus (11:1-44), when Jesus approaches the tomb where the body of his friend Lazarus has been buried for four days. He says to the mourners, "Take away the stone." Martha catches the nonsense of this command and replies: "Lord, there will be a stench."

Yet Jesus' words are clear: *Roll away the stone. Take it away. And you will see the glory of God.*

He is telling Martha, telling the mourning friends of Lazarus, telling you and me: If you want to encounter the glory of God, you have to roll away the stone. You have to remove the seeming impossibilities that stand between you and the glory of God.

Leaning deeply upon his Father's favor, Jesus then prays, "Father, I thank you for hearing me. I know that you always hear me" (11:41-42).

In his own words and actions and expressions of faith, Jesus seems to apprentice his followers here to the far greater encounter they will undergo after his own death and burial. They will encounter the risen One, crucified, buried, and now brought forth from the sealed tomb. They will encounter the One who is the full revelation of the Father's glory.

Yet before we get to Jesus' resurrection, before we even get to his crucifixion and death, we hear him encounter his Father in prayer on other occasions.

After he has spoken to his followers of the grain of wheat which must fall to the ground and die, referring to himself, in order to produce a great yield, he prays: "What should I say? 'Father, save me from this hour'? But it was for this purpose that I came to this hour. Father, glorify your name" (John 12:27-28).

Again he prays, this time openly, unrushed, and at great length, in the hours before his arrest (see John 17). He thanks his Father for the gift which his disciples are, and gives thanks for all those down the ages who will draw close to him and follow him because of their words (see 17:21-24).

And we recall Jesus' anguished prayer in the garden of Gethsemane immediately before his arrest: "Abba, Father, all things are possible for you. Take this cup away from me, but not what I will but what you will" (Mark 14:36).

This prayer encounter in the garden is both moving and instructive: Jesus seems to imagine the possibility that the narrative of his mission might take a different path.

And have I not imagined the same in my own difficult situations?

Yet with an interior surrender which can be described as both obedient and unimaginably gracious, Jesus empties himself of such idle notions and surrenders the total Yes of his being.

Prayer indeed is dynamic encounter. And it is most dynamic when much—or perhaps everything—is at stake. My prayer is most truly dynamic encounter when I am "all in," because God already is "all in."

I discover that dynamic encounter with God must be all, or it is nothing.

What "prayer as dynamic encounter" can look like

Jeremiah, true to his prophetic calling, lived in dynamic relationship with God, a relationship which was both a solemn joy and an interior anguish.

"When I found your words, I devoured them" he says with a prophet's zeal; "they became my joy and the happiness of my heart, / Because I bore your name, / O LORD, God of hosts" (Jeremiah 15:16).

And later, with the same fire-in-the-blood prophetic intensity Jeremiah cries out:

> I say to myself, I will not mention him,
>> I will speak in his name no more.
> But then it becomes like fire burning in my heart,
>> imprisoned in my bones;
> I grow weary holding it in,
>> I cannot endure it. (20:9)

Jeremiah seems impelled to wrestle with his prophetic calling, to resist, to push back from a mission which feels too large for him, too frightening. Yet I sense that it is not his calling that he wrestles with, but with the source of that calling, the very Mystery who is God.

Jacob likewise wrestles in the night with a dark force, a messenger, a man sent by God to deliver both a blessing and a mission (see Genesis 32:23-31). Dynamic encounter in the mystery of dark night.

In prayer which is dynamic encounter I am not the initiator. I am the one who must pay fierce attention to what—or Whom—is greater than me. I must pay fierce attention to the One whom I cannot resist. The One who knows and cherishes my name and who calls me forth in mercy and in love.

I recall, too, an evangelizing missionary with a fiery spirit, the Apostle Paul. In his letter to the Romans, he quotes ancient Moses concerning dynamic encounter with the divine: "The word is near you," he writes, "on your lips, and in your heart" (see Romans 10:8, referring to Deuteronomy 30:14).

The word, the Word, is near you, Paul writes.

On first blush I find this thought consoling. The Word is near me. But instinctively I know that "being near" to the Word is not enough. I cannot endure the gap.

The Word is "on your lips," Paul writes.

On my lips, yes! I experience the Word "on my lips" often. And the Word "on my lips" also is consoling.

Yet this Word which is "on my lips" still is not close enough. Like food, real food and physical nourishment, I cannot settle for the Word being merely "on my lips."

"The Word," Paul finally writes, "is in your heart."

Ah, yes, I say at last. Now, the Word has found its proper home. In my heart, enfleshed. Embedded, even, in the bone, and in the marrow of the bone.

I want this prayer always, dynamic encounter with the Word, prayer which is enfleshed, embedded, alive at the core of my being. Breath of my breath. One heartbeat, not two.

Mature prayer is both an encounter and an indwelling, a decisive and permanent pitching of tents, forming the strong bonds of *communio,* of Beloved Community.

Prayer as dynamic encounter which matures into indwelling might be described in the wise saying I once heard:

> Like the sun and its light,
> the ocean and the wave,
> the singer and the song:
> Not one. But,
> not two.

I discover a maturing here. Not merely a maturing of a prayer life but a maturing of a self-in-God.

What mature prayer requires

Real encounter is a discipline. It is a disciplined way of being in the world. It is a true disciple's way of being in the world. Of being the enfleshed presence of the hidden Christ in the world.

Encountering God, and allowing myself to be encountered by God, is the experience of being truly present. This form of encounter is in fact the inner meaning of "Real Presence."

Such holy encounter captures the hidden universe of meaning embedded in the small yet mighty hyphen which connects I-Thou.

This connection, or at least a deeply sensed intuition, of Real Presence, of I-Thou, is not foreign to the human experience. Why, after all, do people sit and keep vigil with a loved one who is dying? who can no longer communicate? who is more "there" than "here"?

Relationship is real. The conversation continues. Real presence transcends all human capacity for words—whether one is dying, or whether one is just waking up.

Mature prayer as real encounter requires of me the discipline of attentiveness, of intentional acts of paying attention. I discover that I have to be here now. Not here sort of, while also being mostly somewhere else.

Mature prayer as real encounter requires me to notice all the things that are in play: the tone of voice—mine or the other's; the way the eyes meet, or perhaps look just beyond. The laughter, which rises from the belly, or perhaps comes dry, like sawdust, from the throat; the smile, the gestures, generous or constrained.

As I learn how to be present with others in my own unrehearsed daily encounters, so I learn the intentional ways of being present with God in prayer.

And little by little, I discover that mature prayer asks something more of me.

Mature prayer requires of me an ever-expanding capacity for the other. An ever-expanding capacity for God, certainly, and also for the other whom I encounter on the bus, on a sidewalk downtown, in the supermarket, in the course of my work, in my closest relationships, and in the casual and passing ones as well.

As I learn to live generously in my world, and how to respond graciously to the needs of another, which might in fact inconvenience me and stretch me beyond my boundaries of comfort, I learn, little by little, how to make space for all those who are not me—which is everyone.

The disciplined habit of making space for the other whom I see and hear and touch prepares me for a more generous conversation and way of being with God who is beyond my senses.

In other words, my capacity for encounter with the unseen God depends directly on my capacity for encounter with others who are right in front of me.

If I love humanity but cannot stand the individuals whom I meet today, God may have a hard time recognizing me as one made in the divine image and likeness, and capable of divine encounter.

Expanding this interior capacity for the other is a feminine work of the interior life. It is not "women's work" which somehow exempts men from tending to this aspect of the maturing self. But women, perhaps because of a childbearing capacity, may have an enfleshed sense, a genius, a more immediate intuition for what this interior, spiritual work entails.

When I create capacity for the other, I admit what already is most true and most noble about my life: It is not about me. It is about you. Yet the good which you receive cannot happen without me. This mysterious dynamic interaction, which blesses you, also stretches me beyond myself to hold open a space, to actually defend a space, for you.

When I defend a space for you—for your situation—I defend the dignity of your personhood, most especially when you are in need, or fragile, or unfree in some way; when you are most in need of the pure merciful generosity of another human being.

I am free to defend a space for you because God already has defended a space for me. I am free precisely in order to call forth and defend your freedom. My freedom, which flows from God, is for your good.

I think here of the story in Saint Luke's Gospel (10:38-42), when Jesus arrives at the home of his friends Martha and Mary. No doubt he has known good meals here before, lovingly and thoughtfully prepared by Martha. And he has known the joy of spiritually rich conversation with her sister, his disciple Mary.

Perhaps in a moment of sibling discontent, Martha complains to the Lord that her sister should be helping her to prepare the meal, rather than sitting idly at the Master's feet.

And what does Jesus do? He defends Mary's space, and insists, "It will not be taken from her." Here Jesus does this feminine interior work of defending a space for the other, for Mary, who has embraced the role of disciple, typically reserved for men.

Defending a space for prayer

Let's take a closer look at this interior work of creating capacity—of defending a space—for the other.

How often I hear people say, "I would love to have time to pray. But my life is over-scheduled already. I have no way to fit it in."

Truth be told, I have on occasion found myself saying exactly these words about my own life, easily excusing myself from the invitation to prayer.

And here is the spiritual trap: It is not about me "finding" time to pray. It is about acknowledging that the Lord Jesus already is defending ample time for this lovely and intimate encounter. The space already is cleared, held open, prepared, and waiting for me.

Jesus defends this space because it is he who invites me into this most lovely relationship, and into the holy conversation of prayer, at this particular time.

He does not misread my schedule. Nor is he unaware of the endless parade of appointments and commitments and deadlines, and the urgency of it all. The Lord does not get his timing off when he places on my heart the need to pray.

In fact, the Lord's timing on these invitations to prayer is exquisite. Not because prayer is a good thing or even a holy thing. Prayer is the lifeblood of the soul. He knows it, and I know it.

Jesus defends the disciple's necessary spiritual work of "building capacity for the Lord."

He defends my work of setting aside—consecrating—space, and time, for relationship with him, for dwelling in him. Not just for a daily check-in, but for an intentionally nurtured indwelling, a sustained abiding, a deep remaining in him.

Jesus deeply desires to meet me where I am. He also deeply desires for me to meet him where he is.

Another story: Learning to "build capacity for the Lord"

It is a Sunday morning in summer, and all six of us—Mother, Daddy, my three brothers and I—pile into the car. I might be twelve. We are headed south into the valley, and a little west into the hill country, to a little Oregon town called Lafayette, in Yamhill County.

"We are going to Mass someplace different," Mother announces. She is not one to settle for cabin fever. "We are going to the Trappist Abbey."

I have no idea how she learned of this place, or how she knew where to find it. This is an utterly new experience for our family. A new experience for me.

We turn in at the top of the long narrow driveway leading to the abbey. The moss-green buildings nestle peacefully on the shoulder of a wooded hillside.

From the back seat I take in the scenery, the clover and wheat fields in the foreground, the monks' vegetable garden. I notice the way the buildings and the trees and the hillside, the pond, all perfectly fit together, all of it speaking to me a generous and deeply peaceful welcome.

We tiptoe into the dark cool vestibule of the old abbey church. Hushed, we instinctively understand that we have crossed a threshold into sacred space.

Inside, the abbey church exudes an intimacy, a spiritual peace. The entire structure is wood—the rafters, the walls, the choir stalls where the monks gather several times a day, and also in the unseen hours of night, to chant the psalms, and to worship.

I peer through the wood latticework which separates the small lay chapel from the monks' portion of the church. And as I peer through the lattice, down the length of the narrow nave, I espy the monks in their cream-colored choir robes, sitting silently in deep reflection.

My soul belongs here, I think inwardly. My soul has found her home.

Cool breezes waft in from the high transom windows propped open toward the woods. I smell lingering aromas of incense and monk prayer and wood and fresh-baked whole wheat molasses bread.

I breathe in deeply, allowing the aromas to fully embed themselves in my memory.

On cue, the monks in the choir stalls rise form their time of silent prayer and sing the Benedictus, the morning canticle of Zechariah, from Saint Luke's Gospel.

At the end of our pew I catch sight of a small black ring binder. I wonder what this is. So I arise to fetch it and see.

Upon opening this small black binder, I discover that I have found a treasure. It is a collection of the psalms, each page filled with staff lines and those square note shapes and connecting slides which I recognize as Gregorian chant.

I must have this treasure, I think. I must learn how to pray the psalms, pray them always, just as my brother monks pray.

I set the ring binder close to me for now. I wonder how I might procure a copy of my own.

At my young age I know that I have no plan for how I shall pray the psalms, the way my brother monks pray. But something within me knows something. I have no words to describe, or even to properly acknowledge, the gift I have just received, the gift of this ancient form of prayer.

But the invitation has been given. My soul is smitten.

In fact, I discover over time that I feel restless with this invitation to pray the psalms always, just as my brother monks pray.

Through my teen years, in the summer time, we frequently find our way back to the abbey. Silently I feast on the sounds of the monks chanting slowly, softly, the lines of the psalms. I breathe in the sounds, the aromas, the light, the breezes, breathe in until my soul is sated. I do not want to leave.

I befriend a brother monk, or rather, he befriends me. He seems to understand the whole of my unrevealed soul.

He shares with me a small plate of fresh-baked peanut butter cookies. I taste and nearly swoon. I had no idea that monks could bake cookies. My brother monk mails me the recipe, written out in his beautiful cursive hand. I write him back. The friendship is sealed.

And then, one Saturday morning, in my mid twenties, in my little apartment in San Francisco, I hear a knock at my door. A young man, feeling quite awkward with his assignment, apologizes for the interruption. He holds forth a package.

"One of the brothers at Our Lady of Guadalupe Abbey thinks you might need this," he says. He has no idea, I am sure, what he is delivering.

"Thank you," I say. The young man disappears. I close the door and open the package, already suspecting what the gift might be.

Yes, it is a small black ring binder, now my very own copy, of the monks' psalter.

A few paychecks later I walk—no, run—down Geary Street to the music shop, and I purchase a guitar and an instruction book. Quickly I teach myself the chords to the psalm tones which have lingered in my memory.

My apprenticeship in prayer advances to a new level.

Forty years later, still chanting the same psalm tones, with the same guitar, I can say with certainty that the psalms are embedded in my flesh. Lines, stanzas, entire psalms flow freely through my veins, through the marrow of my bones.

So this is what it means, I discover, to build capacity for the Lord. Partly it is about undergoing new experiences—whether I choose them, or whether they choose me.

And in great part, building capacity for the Lord is about letting myself be carried, shaped, invited, haunted, and sated in the soul's irrepressible hunger and thirst for the banquet which is the Lord, utterly sated in his friendship.

Equally, I discover that building capacity for the Lord means intentionally presenting myself to be apprenticed by the Master, to learn how to pray as he prays, so that I can learn how to live as he lives, and to love as he loves.

What do we encounter?

If prayer is "dynamic encounter," and if my prayer, apart from Sunday worship, is a solitary endeavor, what exactly do I encounter?

Rather, Whom, exactly, do I encounter?

Well, God, of course, I could reply. Or I might be more honest and say: I encounter … Mystery.

Yet I want to say that I actually encounter a person.

In my solitary prayer I do indeed encounter another: One whose face I have never seen, whose voice I have never heard. One who lived twenty-one centuries before me. A real flesh-and-blood human being, a man whose feet knew hot sand and cool refreshing streams, whose hands knew the feel of the well-crafted yoke and the sweat of a sun-soaked brow.

In the work of prayer, I notice, one must have either a vivid imagination or pure faith.

Trying to vividly imagine this first-century Jewish man, ultimately, is exhausting for me, and leaves me unsatisfied.

The One whom I seek is not so easily imagined, and not so casually encountered: the crucified Lord and risen Christ. The One who was a holy Fool in service to his Father, whose deepest passion was to reveal the generous, and just, and merciful, and surprising reign of God.

He was so much a holy Fool that he walked straight into the jaws of death, still loving, still entrusting all, right down to his soul, into the hands of his Father.

That's the One whom I encounter. Indescribable, unimaginable. But not unidentifiable. The strong warning of the "doubting" Apostle Thomas calls me up short when I imagine an airbrushed Jesus.

"If you can show me the nail scars, the wound in your side," Thomas says in effect, "then I will worship you."

I will *worship* you.

"If the one you worship has no nail scars," Thomas seems to be warning the Christian community, "that one is not worth following."

The One whom I encounter is God's enfleshed Yes to humanity and to all creation: Jesus, crucified Lord and risen Christ. He is the living One who, Saint Paul insists, "was not alternately Yes and No. He was never anything but Yes" (see 2 Corinthians 1:19).

Christ Jesus, tested and proven worthy of the anointing. Yes, he is the One who makes sense of my suffering, and your suffering, who makes sense of my losses, and your losses.

So this dynamic encounter which I experience in prayer carries me beyond myself, toward the threshold of my self-in-God.

Even, and perhaps, especially in the challenging times, when I am at a loss.

In my prayer, I discover, I am offered not answers to my too-small questions but ... invitations to further apprenticeship.

Specifically, I am offered apprenticeship to a yet fuller and more faithful Gospel way of living. I am apprenticed to deeper forms of leaning in, and listening, and pondering, and then courageously taking the next step.

Prayer, I discover, is the place of invitation—specifically, God's invitation to me to be my authentic self-in-God.

This invitation is important to me. Might it also be important to God?

A closing story: "In you I put my trust"

I recall a time several years ago. I am undergoing severe emotional wounding in the course of my work. I know that I can try to continue to bind up these wounds which I cannot ignore, and duck the constant emotional blows, in order to do the work that is deeply meaningful to me. And to continue also to be gainfully employed.

Or, I can cut myself free from the constant tension of emotional tyranny, and just walk away.

During this season of interior anguish, I recall, late one evening, praying Compline, the church's final prayer of the day. The opening antiphon to the psalm reads: "Do not turn your face from me; in you I put my trust."

For several minutes, sitting at the edge of my bed, I lose myself in the yearning and deep consolation expressed in these words.

"Do not turn your face from me," the soul pleads.

Do not turn away. Do not hide your face. Do not abandon me, O Lord, my God. I have no one but you.

I feel my soul lean deeply into the mystery of this dark space of trust.

After several minutes I return to the words on the page, and begin to pray the psalm.

But I am confused.

This antiphon ... Was it I, speaking these words to the Lord? Or was it he, speaking these words to me?

Do not turn your face from Me. In you I put my trust.

I sit suddenly upright on the edge of my bed, startled with this thought.

In you I put My trust, he seems to say. I trust that you, My beloved, will remain pure in motive, and strong and true, in this time of testing.

Abide with Me. Remain in Me. I am trusting in you. Fix your eyes on Me.

I am startled by such stark poverty, the poverty of Love which never coerces but which only invites, beckons, pleads, knowing that the beloved, in weakness or discouragement, might cave in or simply turn away.

In this moment I instinctively understand that my work, my larger assignment, lies beyond this time of testing. These are the birthing pains, I discover, the pains of a certain form of dying, so that something greater can be born.

Questions for Reflection, Journaling,
or Conversation

Looking back

What insights into "prayer as encounter" have been meaningful for me? Which phrases speak to me? Which images?

What experiences of "prayer as encounter" in my own life come to mind—from my earlier years, from the middle span of time, or from the present or recent past?

How might the Lord be apprenticing me in the ways of prayer as encounter? How would I describe this apprenticeship?

Looking forward

How might I apply these insights into prayer, to more deeply form my own prayer practices?

What word, or phrase, or insight, seems to be the gift that will carry me forward?

The prayer that comes to me now …

PART 2

THE INTIMATE CONVERSATION OF HOLY TRINITY
Prayer as holy conversation

On my prayer table, in the predawn flickering light of a small oil lamp, I gaze upon a large icon of Holy Trinity. The serenity of these three figures seated at table permeates the room with an air of peace.

An opening reflection: Holy Trinity

So much so, this peace, that the rooms of my living quarters could never abide the sound of a television, nor the sounds of quarreling, or discord.

This sacred icon of Holy Trinity has come to define my space, my spirit, my interior disposition.

Written by sixteenth-century Russian monk Andrei Rublev for the edification of his brother monks, this icon expresses the one holy and endless conversation of Love.

The figure in the center of this icon, the figure which first captures the eye, is the Son. Two elements reveal his identity: the rabbi robe, certainly, in its earthy tones, and also those extended two fingers of the right hand which rests discreetly on the table. The middle and index fingers speak in simple gesture the Son's identity: human, and divine.

This subtle gesture of two fingers extended is meant for me, I sense—the Son communicating directly to me this astonishing truth of who he is—while he gazes with everlasting love upon the Father.

I gaze upon the Son beholding the Father. No words spoken in this beholding; simply a holy, penetrating, and everlasting gaze of love.

I notice that the Father, seated to the left, does not, in return, gaze upon the Son but upon the figure on the right, the Holy Spirit. Here too, between them, I behold a holy, penetrating, and everlasting gaze of love.

The Father, represented here, is no imposing figure. In fact, in facial features, in physical bearing, Father seems indistinguishable from Son and Holy Spirit. The three faces, I notice, are the same serene and contemplative face. A serene and feminine face.

Now my eye is drawn to another detail. I notice that Father and Holy Spirit are barefoot, suggesting to me an unguarded humility. Their feet, in fact, seem ready to dance lightly, spritely.

If Son is gazing in everlasting love upon Father, and if Father is gazing in everlasting love upon Holy Spirit, then where does Holy Spirit gaze?

Downward, serenely, into middle space, into the space where all the holy ones dwell. Where you and I dwell. Where our forebears dwell, and all who will come after us.

In subtle gesture of benediction, this Advocate whom Jesus promised seems to bless the world, lovingly, everlastingly, with hand extended as though in a gesture of divine protection.

The words of Psalm 19 come to mind: "No speech, no word, no voice is heard." As I behold this sacred icon I hear no speech, no word, no voice. Yet I am drawn irresistibly, deeply, into the eternal holy conversation of Holy Trinity.

And this eternal holy conversation is love. It is *about* love, yes. But the conversation *is* love. An eternal expression of love, yes, but closer still: The holy conversation of Holy Trinity is, simply ... Love.

Words fail. Language collapses. I can only gaze into this one holy conversation. A gaze which is a pure form of entry into holy Mystery.

To behold one of the Three, I discover, is to behold all three in the eternal holy conversation which is Love.

And now, in the foreground of this table of divine banquet, what do I find? I see a golden broad-bowled cup, containing something dark, the color of wine.

But it is not wine. Bread, perhaps?

No, it is not bread. If you look closely, if you look with a magnifying glass, you will find that this broad-bowled cup contains ... the sacrificial Lamb.

This simple vessel in the foreground stands out distinctly against the light-mottled backdrop of the table's surface.

How did I overlook this detail for so long? My attention shifts, from the three serene faces deep in loving gaze to this cup of Sacrifice, now the blazing focus of my attention.

The cup, too, I discover, is part of this holy conversation. The cup is the communication of Love. This cup, bearing the sacrificial Lamb, is a complete sentence. It is the one sentence. It is the Word, really, which is *with* God, and which *is* God.

I suddenly realize that this cup, bearing the sacrificial Lamb, this one complete sentence, is all that God has ever communicated, and ever will.

What more could God ever possibly need to say?

The cup, bearing the sacrificial Lamb, is God's complete outpouring of self. In our stumbling and imperfect language we call this outpouring: Mercy.

Love pours out, and I am invited in.

And this open space in the foreground, this open space which I had not considered, I now realize is the space reserved at table for me. And for you. Everlastingly reserved, personally, uniquely.

It is the open space of invitation, the one invitation that carries the holy urgency of Love's yearning, in the Son's words, "that all might be one in us."

The invitation to be at this table now, everlastingly. To enter into the intimate conversation of Holy Trinity, and not go away. Ever.

It is the one holy invitation which I cannot refuse. And which, honestly, you cannot refuse.

We are invited, you and I, to enter into this wordless holy conversation. To turn *from* the world of chaos and many things, and to turn *toward* and *into* the divine *communio* of peace and the one thing.

I have not yet found the perfect word that would describe the one thing. But I partake it already. Little by little I undergo a decisive shift, from many disparate things to the one thing, from exclusion to inclusion. From chaos and distraction to a radical holy simplicity.

Heaven begins. Resurrection finds purchase in mortal flesh, and bone, and blood. Resurrection finds purchase in graced ways of being.

The eternal divine banquet is now.

An opening Scripture: Luke 11:1-4
"Lord, teach us to pray"

"He was praying in a certain place," Saint Luke narrates in the course of Jesus' ministry.

Jesus' disciples perhaps are accustomed to the Master's habit of going to "a certain place," perhaps for extended periods of time. Often in the night, but perhaps also in the course of a day.

Here they are, surely wanting to press ahead before the day grows hot. And they are stalled, again, because the Master is in prayer.

Yet even here the Teacher is at work. His habit of prayer, his "going to a certain place to pray," is in fact the start of their apprenticeship in prayer. Jesus' habit of prayer—the actual practice of prayer, his persistence in prayer, and the effects of prayer on his life and mission— likely stirs in his disciples a hunger to embrace this habit, too.

And one of his disciples says to him, "Lord, teach us to pray, as John has taught his disciples."

No doubt these disciples of Jesus and of John knew each other, or at least observed each other from a distance and noted each other's progress. Their classroom was not within the walls of rabbi school but in the open spaces, in public places.

So Jesus begins to teach his followers what he himself knows of prayer. He invites them into a deeper phase of discipleship.

"Learn from *me,*" he seems to say here. Not just from my words but from my disposition of heart.

At the one disciple's request Jesus replies to all of his disciples: "When you pray, say these words ..."

When Jesus tells me, his twenty-first century disciple, " ... say these words," I know that I must pay very close attention—not just to get the words right, but to enter into the relationship of trust and accountability with his Father which these words evoke.

"Father," Jesus begins.

In Luke's Gospel, the prayer opens with a simple, courteous address.

In Matthew's Gospel we hear the words "Our Father." *Our* Father— a phrase which includes, and presumes, community.

Now I speak the word *Father,* and in so doing I acknowledge the relationship which already exists. Father. Abba. Papa. And who is it who calls out these words? Daughter, beloved child, your little one.

"Father," the daughter prays.

The heart of one calls upon the heart of the Other.

And now Jesus follows the opening address to the Father with the lovely phrase, " ... hallowed be your name."

Yes, to address God, and now to speak a lovely attribute of God: *Holy is your name*. This too is courteous, and engages me deeply, immediately, in this one relationship which gives shape and meaning to all others.

I speak this word *Holy* and I tumble headlong, soul-first, into an abyss of adoration.

Holy ... holy ... holy ...

I speak these words. Or, more accurately, I silently hold space for these words to come forth, and the soul falls into realms of worship outside of time. Not by my doing, but by the sway of grace.

Holy. Not merely one among many attributes of God, but the very essence of God. Holy is the very essence of what I must become, since I am from God, and my life also is a journeying into to God.

The holiness of God, I discover, is my native home, where I am most myself. Yet the recalcitrant wanderer in me too quickly forgets.

Holy is your name, I pray. Now, yes, in this place and time. But the words point my heart and mind and spirit toward a full insistence that God's name be held holy, always.

And now Jesus gives his disciples the beautiful words, "Your kingdom come."

Your kingdom, your reign, come! *Your* reign.

Not the reign of Caesar. Not the reign of Empire. Not the reign of my oh-so-logical and lovingly crafted plans. *Your* reign. The reign of GOD.

Bold words, these, which press hard against the tide of mortal hubris and human ingenuity.

I sense an urgency in this first petition of the Lord's Prayer. In fact, I sense that this first petition is the complete and perfect petition: Your kingdom come.

This first petition speaks the one desiring that encompasses all the desirings of the Father's heart. And therefore it calls forth the purest and most earnest desirings of the heart of humankind.

Come, reign of All Good which blesses everyone, which blesses all of creation!

"Restore us to the Garden," this first petition seems to say, where we can truly be, together, the image of God, and this time get it right.

Luke's version of the Lord's prayer moves now to the next petition: "Give us each day our daily bread."

Asking God for daily bread is, for most people I know, a quaint notion. When I need bread, I bake it. Most people I know buy it.

I have no idea what it is like to career from day to day, not knowing where my next meal will come from, or how I will feed a hungry family.

How easily, unthinkingly, I pray these words: Give us each day our daily bread.

What's to pray for here, really? Quite a lot.

This petition in the Lord's Prayer is not so much about bread, or lack of bread. This petition is about openly acknowledging that, by virtue of my being human, I live a precarious life, no matter how much wealth I have socked away.

And therefore, no matter my wealth, I must live with complete trust in God—as the norm. GOD is my God, not my wealth.

This petition speaks a willingness to live at the edge, with a deep and sobering and humble acceptance that everything, in a heartbeat, could be otherwise, that all is grace. Not human ingenuity, or smart planning, but grace.

This petition calls me to an honest gospel poverty, to live open to the possibility of pernicious uncertainty, the uncertainty with which many people live whose stinking poverty is so painfully obvious to me.

Openly and publicly acknowledging my precarity, I discover, is an effective antidote to pride in self-sufficiency.

So the sobering question is this: Am I ready to pray this petition, and to mean it deeply? Am I ready to lean hard into God, not on my terms but on God's terms, in this life which is fragile and contingent on forces beyond me? To live the way Jesus actually lived?

And now, without pausing for breath, the Master continues: "and forgive us our sins." No comma, no pause. Give us and forgive us. Give and forgive. Please, Abba!

And even here the Master does not pause: "Give us … and forgive us, … for we ourselves forgive."

He gives us a lot to digest here, if we were to mindfully chew on each phrase.

The logic of the spiritual life, Jesus seems to say, is this: I cannot receive forgiveness as long as I am holding a grudge. I can hold the grudge, or I can drop the grudge and open my arms to forgiveness. But I cannot do both.

This petition, about forgiveness, actually is about me. The focus here is not so much my dependence on God but my willingness to undergo conversion, from self-righteousness to unexplainable mercy.

I would be lying if I were to stand before God and say that I am that forgiving person.

Forgive me, Father, to the extent that I forgive the one toward whom I am least forgiving. The one for whom I cut the least slack. The one I am quick to judge, and in whom I find a certain righteous satisfaction in judging. After all …

Such logic arms the soul against grace.

When I forgive and let go what I would rather hold against another, I increase my capacity to receive what God desires to give me. Receiving God's grace and good clearly depends on my willing to let go.

Not that I merit God's grace and good. But my arms, and my heart, become free to receive.

Forgive us as we forgive, the petition says. Forgive me as I forgive.

In this petition Jesus, most excellent Teacher, holds his followers to a higher standard than we would willingly choose for ourselves. Across the four Gospels, we hear Jesus use the word *forgive,* or its variants, forty times. Even as he undergoes a hideous public crucifixion he cries out to his Father to forgive his executioners.

I am sobered. And convicted. I know that I cannot pray this petition lightly, or dismissively, or even unthinkingly.

And finally, the Teacher instructs his disciples to pray for what he himself surely prays for: "Do not subject us to the final test."

The final test, for early hearers of the gospel, could mean the trials of the much anticipated end times.

Yet for us, as it was for Jesus, the final test, the final temptation, is personal. Later in Luke's Gospel, in extreme agony at the Mount of Olives, Jesus again tells his followers, "Pray that you may not undergo the test" (Luke 22:40).

You recall the scene. On that dark night of his arrest Jesus prays: "Father, if you are willing, take this cup away from me. Still, not my willing, but yours." So earnest is his prayer that he is visited by an angel as he prays, his sweat becoming "like drops of blood falling on the ground" (Luke 22:42-44).

The final test. The final exam. Everything, I discover, rides on the arc of my apprenticeship. Everything depends on how well I have paid attention, how fully I have given myself all along to the mission entrusted to me.

The Lord's Prayer is not complex. It is not over worded. In clean and simple phrases it goes straight to the point, expressing in useful words the nature of this one relationship which gives context and purpose to all other relationships.

This prayer carries me to the very heart of Jesus' own relationship with his Father.

Each petition, I discover, when prayed in a heartfelt way, requires something of me as much as it asks something of God. I discover that I must continually expand my interior capacity for God, for the petitions to be fulfilled in me.

The Lord's Prayer, I find, becomes my personal invitation to enter into the holiness of God. To enter into the one holy conversation which is beyond me, yet which includes me.

A meditation on two words

I have long understood that, eventually, words will fail me.

A strange thought, I notice, for one whose life's work is shaped by words.

Yet words, in the end, will fail me, the way that words fail the Master in his final discourse in the hours before his arrest. He struggles to express ultimate things within the constraints of human language. And the language simply collapses.

I in them; You in me; I dwelling in You; that they all may be one as we are one.

Words get in the way, sometimes, because the best words, the few and necessary words, are indeed about ultimate things. Yet words, I discover, can drain the life out of prayer.

I have a hunch that, in the end, even the few and necessary words will come down to the one Word, in whom all things hold together.

This morning I rise at four-fifteen for my weekly early sitting with the Lord in silent prayer, before the start of Morning Prayer.

I bring every good intention into this quiet space, and for forty-five minutes I chase after the peace and settledness of the deep *communio* which I so earnestly desire to experience in this silent time.

I know that I am trying too hard. My mind feels frenzied. So I pull back and let it be. Just … let it be.

Just … be.

I sense that even clods of cool earth under the starry night sky can "just ... be" more gracefully than I am in this early morning struggle toward silence.

Simplify, I hear the interior voice say. Just breathe, and simplify.

And in a quiet burst of gratitude I remember and return to the one word which for me is the complete and perfect prayer.

The one word which is the Name above every other name: *Jesus.*

Over the years this most holy Name, which is complete and perfect prayer, has instructed me in how it wishes to be prayed. Not springing from the lips, not generating from the throat, the vocal cords.

No. This holy Name, which is the fullness of prayer, insists on rising up from the soles of my feet, moving inward from the outer edges of my physical being, through every pore of skin, moving inward to infuse and enlighten and animate every cell of my being, every cell of muscle and blood, and bone, and marrow of bone.

The holy Name claiming every corner of the temple, the entire space of worship, which is the entirety of my being.

And now the name comes forth as prayer: *Jesus.*

The Name, which is the one beautiful Word.

It rolls outward, unstoppable as a tidal wave, crashing over the jagged rock formations and massive driftwood logs of interior self, and ebbing back toward the inky silent mystery of sea.

I sit, stunned by the power of this one Word which prays itself through me, the Name which is the tidal force of worship of the Father.

The temple is prayed through, I discover, the temple of my being. A temple too small, its walls too porous, to contain the mighty worship which is the Name above and beyond and before every other name.

I sit, stunned and washed clean, and purified, by the divine force which has welled up from the depths and washed through me. For several minutes I sit, wordless, as the Word prays lingeringly through me. Like the lingering smoke of now-spent incense.

Outside I hear the shrill and distant cry of a swallow making its first foray through the predawn sky, catching in midair, I imagine, the day's first batch of hatchling flies.

I cannot make prayer happen. But I can present myself as the temple through which the Word prays in worship to the Father.

I rest a moment, and let the residue foam of grace also rest on the sea-drenched sand of soul.

Now, from the eastern edge of my south-facing window, up in the corner, where the mountain ash tree canopy gives way to open sky, I see the first delicate trace of dawn.

Still aware of my good intentions and utter inability to make prayer happen, resisting thoughts of all that I need—or at least desire—to accomplish today, I pull back and open up space for the next wave of prayer to wash through me.

A word begins to form, a second word, a simple utterance of the soul. A simple word, not complex, not explained or embellished or qualified.

A word begins to form which is the unguarded, fearless expression of self-offering. The expression of pure and total trust.

The word comes forth, impelled by the hidden grace of joy: *Yes!*

This beautiful word hangs in mid-air, diminishing ever so gently, like a pure solitary note plucked from a harp string: *Yes!*

There. I said it. The complete one-word sentence. The word which also comes like a tidal wave, rolling and rushing with a mighty force, only to spend itself utterly upon the shore of my being.

Yes, I pray, and know that the world, and the lives I touch today, will all somehow participate in revealing, in some way, the desiring and mercy and goodness of God.

Yes, I pray. And I accept with relief and gratitude that all language, all striving and all intention, even, collapses in the effort to express in human terms this one ultimate necessity: life lived in God.

What might this word *Yes* mean?

In its deepest expression, *Yes* is a spiritual word. And as a spiritual word it is not one that expresses the confidence of knowing, the false confidence of self-assuredness.

Rather, it is a word of assent, a word that emerges from a place of not-knowing, from a place of radical trust.

I think of the young Mary of Nazareth, turning in her heart toward her betrothed, with an image of married life sweet in her mind.

And from beyond the horizon of her understanding irrupts an invitation to a distinctly different narrative, a unique invitation that will utterly reshape not only her life but the lives of many down through the generations.

And to this astonishing invitation she says: *Yes!*

Not because she is given a map for this extraordinary journey. No map is offered.

She is free to say *Yes* because she already is in relationship with the Almighty "who is doing great things for me."

Like Mary, I am free to say *Yes* to the Almighty who is doing great things for me, and through me, when I give myself to the relationship.

I must open the space, actively defend a space, for the unexpected yet long-sought invitations to arrive.

In fact, I have to *be* "Yes" before I can *say* "Yes" to the invitations which God has in mind. I must *do* "Yes." I must live as though my life already is this one-word prayer.

A story: "Saying *Yes* before I know the details"

Back in my late twenties, early thirties, I suddenly sprout a hunch, an intuition, that I need to work in some way in service to church.

I have no idea where this notion comes from, because it has not been a part of my life so far.

And now, moving forward some twenty years, in my early fifties, with two parish jobs in my rear view mirror, and finding no positions for church work posted anywhere in the region, I find myself captive to what the Lord might have in mind.

I find myself captive, actually, to the wordless conversation of Holy Trinity, the wordless conversation I have beheld in the sacred icon on my prayer table.

An invitation comes in the form of an e-mail from my brother about a job posting that caught his eye.

"It's not exactly the kind of work you are looking for," he cautions me. "Nor is it in a part of the country you would ever think to live."

But I know that I need to pay attention to the invitation, because, I remind myself, you just never know how one thing might lead to another.

Within two weeks I fly eastward for an interview, and return home with an offer in my pocket. Within a month I breathlessly pull up my fifth-generation Oregon roots to move across the Rockies to the wide-open prairie.

The job description to which I have said *Yes* matches the script in the classified ad.

The actual assignment to which I have said *Yes* is yet to be revealed.

For the next two and a half years I reach daily into the depths of soul and spirit to give my *Yes* to what often feels like an excruciating encounter with dark and hostile forces.

Only far into the assignment do I discover that my real reason for being there is to bring to light what has been hiding in the dark. To call out and to challenge what has grown comfortably underground.

And I become sharply aware that my continuing *Yes* to this assignment will eventually cost me my job.

Indeed, the day arrives when I am set free of my duties.

I walk away feeling ... not angry but light, the chafing yoke lifted.

I am unburdened of salary and health insurance, to be sure. But I am unburdened, also, the way I imagine the soul of the crucified Lord must have felt in the cool quiet space of the tomb. The strife is over. The assignment, completed.

So I return to my beloved Oregon, to the town, and the same part of town, where I lived before. Not because any new offer of employment awaits me, but because at least I have my people.

And now, at the same prayer table, before the same beloved icon of Holy Trinity, my boxes not yet unpacked, with no job prospects or employment opportunities lined up, I kneel in prayer. And again I pray my *Yes* to the One who I know will arrive from the farthest horizon to deliver fresh invitations.

Yes, I discover, can be prayed only when soul and heart and mind and spirit are emptied of expectations. Emptied of worry. Emptied of all that would distract the interior self, or pull it off its mission.

The importance of noticing things: Antidote to an overstimulated culture

Something sublimely countercultural happens when I meditate upon the sacred icon of Holy Trinity.

Noise stops. Clutter falls away. The endless press of all that seems so urgent evaporates in the presence of the one eternal conversation of Father, Son, and Holy Spirit.

The great weight of all that is not important falls away, as the soul enters into this divine *communio.*

Yet one thing becomes all the more important: the holy work of noticing things.

Noticing the particulars, the subtle presences, the overlooked details, the missed nuances of the ordinary, of the commonplace, the taken-for-granted.

If I love God, I notice, then I have to love what God loves.

If I love Jesus, then I have to love what Jesus loves. And I have to allow my heart to break over those things that break his heart first.

Which means that I have to pay attention to what in the world is going on. I have to pay attention to what in *my* world is going on.

As many people do, I pray as I walk.

For me, this is not necessarily prayer which carries the urgency of petition. Nor does it have the feel of ongoing conversation between friends.

Oftentimes when I walk I experience prayer which rises up as pure astonishment of this deep red rose whose stem bends with the weight of the bloom over the sidewalk where I pass. Yes, this particular red rose whose fragrance ran to meet me several paces back.

I experience prayer which rises up as humble gratitude toward the ruffian-looking youth who sits one seat ahead of me on the bus, and who leaps forward to flip back the bank of side-facing seats to make way for a wheelchair-boarding passenger.

I experience prayer which rises up as mercy as I look into the weathered face and sad eyes of Gloria who lives in her car and who is "here" because she can no longer be "there," and who feels hopeful about things—which she cannot specifically name—because she knows that God is with her.

I notice Gloria's thin lips, and her teeth, and the gaps in between where teeth used to be.

I notice the day-old odor as the ruffian-looking youth one seat ahead of me sits down again.

I notice the warmth of sunlight which draws forth the intoxicating fragrance of the deep red rose.

I notice, right now, the endless squawking of the scrub jay family as they claim my yard as their territory, theirs alone, and all lesser birds are put on notice. Their squawking, which tears away any semblance of peace most hours of every day, expands my heart to love even these birds, bullies, nest robbers, mockers of sanity. These scrub jays upon whom God casts a loving eye.

I notice things, and therefore I pray.

I notice the two deadly shooting sprees last week which have brought the nation, again, to a place of shock and grief. And I notice, as the eucharist gifts are brought up on Sunday morning, two carafes of wine, not one, as though human blood poured out, twice now in this week, becomes the matter of our eucharistic offering.

I pray because I notice things, all around me. Not everything, not all things, but the things that God would have me notice, in order to expand the conversation of Holy Trinity within my heart.

When I notice what God would have me notice, I learn how to know and to love and to care for the things that God knows and loves and cares for.

Noticing things, in short, leads me to active engagement in my world, in this world which God still so loves. My noticing things matters to God, because God cares for the particulars. And so it matters to me, so that I too might care for the particulars.

The discipline of noticing things: Paying attention

But noticing things does not simply happen. I can give away my TV (which I did), avoid the disorienting lure of department stores and shopping malls (which I do), and disencumber myself of a car and all the costly maintenance and insurance and repairs, and the need to earn enough after-tax money to pay for it all (which I also have done).

But these actions, decisive as they are, do not lead me to pray.

Prayer, or intentional deep entry into the holy conversation of Holy Trinity, is a discipline. I must forsake the distractions in order to enter, interiorly composed and wholehearted, into the house of God. I must be discipled in the art and ways of that deeper conversation, which is the one conversation that really matters: the holy conversation, which is Love.

With endless distractions in an overstimulated world, I find myself bombarded with eye candy, ear candy, brain candy, recreational shopping, a carefree life, and those daily little splurges "just because."

I find myself swimming in a culture of addiction to whatever will buffer me from what I do not want to face. Whatever will buffer me from those deeper invitations to "something more."

I feel exhausted, living in a culture that runs so hard, so fast, and that works so feverishly to avoid embracing the radical—and original— simplicity of dwelling in God.

"Fix your eyes on the One who calls you," I remind myself often, the way Peter, in the frenzy of the storm, fixes his eyes on his Lord.

Listen for his voice, I remind myself. Listen for his invitation. Fix your eyes. Listen. Put one foot in front of the other. Do not look down at the impossibility of it all. Do not look back. Fix your eyes, your intention, your heart, on the One who calls you.

All of this listening and fixing the eyes and taking one step and then another is pure discipline. No one can do it for me, I discover. There are no shortcuts. There is no downloadable app to make it easy.

There is only the wholehearted embrace of apprenticeship to an encounter, a relationship, a holy conversation, a way of life far richer than what I alone can craft.

And the invitations to this way of life in God are everywhere. All I have to do is pay attention. Pay fierce attention. To the One who calls me.

"If you love father or mother or the comforts and safe parameters of home," Jesus warns, "you are not worthy of me."

He says, "You have to be willing, … willing to lay it all down."

Those who are courageous enough to apprentice to the Lord must not only be willing to lay it all down. They have to actually lay it all down.

Apprenticing to the Lord, I discover, requires not only intention but action.

I can stand at the bus stop on a Sunday afternoon with that one last sandwich in my backpack which I am holding back for my lunch. Or I can turn and take two steps to my left, say hello to the tired old gent in the green sweater-vest who also is waiting for the bus, ask him how he's doing today, and gently ask if he has had anything to eat.

I am pretty sure he hasn't. So I hand him my lunch.

Paying attention to what is right beside me, two feet away from my skin, I discover, is the shortest route to heaven.

Paying attention, letting myself be gently nudged and guided by the Holy Spirit, and then doing the next obvious thing, is the three-step dance into the banquet room of Holy Trinity.

There are no shortcuts to paying attention. I live in a world defined by space and time, by circumstances and constant change, by precarity which admits no guarantees of safety or success.

My intentional act of paying attention becomes the open portal through which the Spirit of the risen Christ enters, in order to touch lives, heal the world, and reveal the reign of God—through me.

This discipline of noticing things bends the heart toward compassion. And I admit: I am not, by nature, an overly compassionate person. So I discover that acts of compassion become an inescapable invitation to my own conversion of heart.

"If you want to be close to Me," the Lord whispers, "get close to that man sitting with his bedroll—yes, that one, with the matted hair, sitting on the bench outside the library."

Or, "If you want to share the divine banquet with us," Holy Trinity whispers, "offer your sandwiches and bottles of water to these three young street people, sitting on their coats around that lamppost across the intersection."

How did I get into this practice of roaming around downtown on Sunday afternoons? What was I thinking? I could be enjoying a leisurely lunch with friends, or tending to gardening chores in my back yard.

All I can say is that paying attention to things, paying attention to what is going on in my world, changes me. Because I really do desire to put my heart with the heart of God.

Apprenticing into the larger conversation of your life

I distinctly recall an image which I had of myself, which I carried with me throughout my twenties.

I am sitting in a chair, a simple bentwood chair, in an empty room. I am waiting, for what I do not know. Simply waiting. Not looking about. (What is there to engage my attention in an empty room?) I am just waiting. Not agitated with having to wait, alone in this bare room. Just … waiting.

And I distinctly recall the conversation of my twenties. It is conversation with God. In the early light of dawn, in the starry hours of night, I pour heart and soul into the conversation of the Psalms—which is Jesus' conversation with his Father, the soul's conversation with God.

In this tender decade of my twenties, this conversation grows deeply meaningful for me. Not because Jesus is my friend. I seem unable to regard him in this way.

This conversation grows deeply meaningful for me because, even in my twenties, I intuit that God alone can hold the mystery of my life.

I have no vision for this life. I trust that God holds the vision. And I trust that God is perfectly fine with my not having the vision.

It is a conversation of trust and consolation, because in this early season of my life I feel so terribly alone.

As I move toward my thirties I feel an unexplainable itch to leave my job as a legal secretary—certainly work for which I have felt grateful, and to which I have applied myself wholeheartedly.

Yet I feel the itch to leave this work behind, in order to pursue graduate studies in … theology.

I have no idea where this itch has come from. Nor have I any idea what I will do with this degree. No vision, no plan. Yet even though I cannot name it, a new apprenticeship has begun.

Once I enter graduate school I notice that all kinds of doors and windows begin to open for me, drawing me into friendships and rich immersion into Christian community, now with Franciscan characteristics; drawing me toward broader horizons where fresh invitations, unnamable as yet, await me.

I feel irresistibly drawn toward God who is passionately involved in the world's suffering, the world's wonder, and the world's hope.

But when my studies are over, I learn that the internship I had counted on goes to someone else. I do not graduate. I go adrift. One thing leads to another, though not to any roles in service to church.

My thirties roll into my forties. My forties roll by. The image of the solitary young woman sitting in her simple bentwood chair is replaced now by the frenzy of a responsible adult life.

I still have no vision, really, for what this life might become.

The next phase of apprenticeship begins when, again, I am working, now for the management team of a small manufacturing firm. Again, I feel grateful for my work, and apply myself wholeheartedly to the assignment.

And again, I am visited by an unexplainable itch, and feel the inescapable invitation to finish my theology degree, which I abandoned seventeen years earlier. I feel the itch to leave this job, to untether myself and make myself truly available to what God might have in mind.

The time to untether has not yet arrived, but the itch remains strong.

I have no idea what these unexplainable itches mean. But I am keenly aware that something within me knows something. I feel as though I am in a room where a conversation is going on, a conversation that involves me, my future, my life, but a conversation which I am not invited to enter.

I pick up the thread of my graduate studies. My interest picks up. My studies find their focus. I begin to feel engaged in my life in an entirely new way, a way that now seems open to possibilities which are not my doing but God's.

I complete my degree. I leave my full-time job. I hoist one leg and then the other over the side of the boat, and begin to walk across the uncertain surface of my life toward the One who calls me.

The One who calls me does not share with me the plan. But I can tell, by the dancing way his eyes sparkle their light into my eyes, that indeed he has a plan, and that I can be joyful and confident in moving toward him across the uncertain surface.

How do you apprentice into the larger conversation of your life?

First, I have learned, you have to let go the notion that you have a plan. You place yourself under the care of the Master who knows you intimately and loves you intensely. Who has a knack for calling forth the potential within you, so that his intense love can reach those whose lives you will touch.

Second, I have learned, you have to let go the "yes buts." The Master is very clear: Leave behind your attachments to father and mother, to a comfortable life; let go your sandals, your second tunic, your walking stick. Your wallet.

Or, be like Elisha. Slaughter your twelve yoke of oxen, and set fire to your work tools in order to boil the water that will roast the ox flesh for your final meal with family. Be done with what once sustained you and move toward what is big enough to hold you now, toward what calls you, whether you can name it or not.

Let go your illusions of security, of success, of greatness. Let go, even, of your need for recognition for all you are sacrificing. You have to let go.

"Lose your life in order to find it," the Master says. He speaks with an authority that will chasten you.

Third, you apprentice into the larger conversation of your life by trusting—deeply trusting and accepting—that your life is about far more than you. That you are not hermetically sealed against the concerns and harsher edges of the world in which you live. You will be not only changed but sometimes inconvenienced. And sometimes sorely tested.

By virtue of your share in a common humanity, and even more so by virtue of your anointing, your life is part of the larger conversation of the world's creativity and suffering and hope. You are part of the world's life, its striving, its anguish, its dying, and its coming to new life.

It's this "accepting" part that can be most challenging. When one corner of the world, or of the nation, or even one corner of your town, plunges into an abyss of chaos and anguish, you can refuse to enter into that conversation. Or you can reach into the depths of your own humanity and find a way to be part of the necessary and graced response.

And it's the "accepting" part, accepting that your life is about far more than you, that enables you to eventually graduate from the apprenticeship class into active apostleship.

And isn't apostleship the point of your anointing?

What I keep learning, in endlessly new ways, is that I do not choose the form or content, or even the timing, of my apprenticeship; the Lord does. Nor do I choose the forms of apostleship; the Lord does.

I do not choose these larger conversations of my life. They choose me, just as they choose you. And as Jesus promised, the Holy Spirit will give each of us words to speak when it is time for us to speak them. Thankfully.

Prayer: A way of being in conversation with God

Early seventeenth-century Anglican vicar and poet George Herbert writes that prayer is "the soul in paraphrase." Or, the soul "in other words."

Prayer, the poet suggests, is not the longings or the hopes of the soul, but the soul itself, "in words."

Or, sometimes, not words. But always words—or, not words— addressed to another, addressed to a Thou.

For some people, these are words addressed to the God of their understanding.

I prefer to address my words to God who is beyond my understanding.

Not words spoken into a dark and distant void, but spoken to the One who is nearer to me than I am to myself. The One, therefore, whom I cannot see. The One who is Mystery, and also Soul of my soul, Breath of my breath, Flesh and Blood of my own flesh and blood.

So I am speaking of prayer which is more a way of "being present" than it is "having a way with words."

Words, in fact, can be a benefit to me, helping me to come to just the right spare expression of God's view of the matter of my prayer and the concerns of my heart.

Words, in prayer, those few lean and necessary words which emerge as a fruit of silence and stillness before the Lord, help me to discern God's willing, God's desiring.

In essence, words, in prayer, become a gentle process by which my heart and mind and soul and attitude become conformed to Christ. Using only those few lean words I discover that I "speak" my way into the Mystery who is God.

Not words of my choosing, but the words which the Holy Spirit prays through me. For I do not know, really, how to pray as I ought.

This dialogue with God, who is Mystery, the wholly Other who also is Soul of my soul, Breath of my breath, Flesh and Blood of my own flesh and blood, *this* holy dialogue is a way of being in relationship.

So prayer, I discover, is a way of being in relationship with God.

Being in conversation with God, in prayer, means encountering God, who is Mystery.

And being in conversation with God also means being encountered by this One who is Mystery, yet who also is Soul of my soul, Breath of my breath, Flesh and Blood of my own flesh and blood.

When I enter into this holy dialogue of prayer, I encounter not only God who is Mystery, but I encounter also the dignity of my being-in-God, the dignity of my humanity, my personhood.

My prayer, I discover, which I express only at the prompting of the Holy Spirit, calls forth a sure dignity and benediction for my fruitful participation in the reign of God.

In my prayer I become the channel through which the Holy Spirit intercedes to the Father, and the channel through which the Father, in great love, communicates to the Son the holy desiring for my life.

And the Son, who is my Way and my Truth and my Life, opens the door of my heart, my understanding, the door of my capacities and my ability to pay attention, opens up my ability to notice things, to connect the dots, and to take right action.

A true story: "Bring in a management team"

I am in Morning Prayer, just as I am, faithfully, every morning.

And I find myself in a season, which by now has spanned a few years, when I feel like I am pushing water uphill. The speaking and writing ministry I am trying to put together seems to be going nowhere. My phone does not ring, the contracts do not come in.

On this morning I finally admit my exhaustion and, quite frankly, my discouragement. "How long, O Lord," the Psalmist cries, and I feel deeply the longing in the anguished cry.

And then, cartoon-like, a thought balloon pops into place beside my head: "Bring in a management team," it says.

I cannot even think of bringing in a management team. I do not have the money. I dismiss the idea and return my attention to my Morning Prayer.

A new thought balloon pops up: "Bring in the best management team there is."

Hmmm, I think. This notion seems persistent. I am not thinking about hiring a management team, so I wonder what these messages mean.

Well, I can think of one management team. Very smart, very respected, very successful. Very much beyond my reach. I dismiss the thought and return to my Morning Prayer.

A third time a thought balloon pops into place: *"Bring in Holy Trinity!"*

I throw my head back in laughter, because it all instantly makes sense. My eyes go immediately to the large icon right before me on the prayer table, the sacred icon of Holy Trinity.

In a flash I understand: The Father is the visionary. The Son is the chief operations officer, to whom I report directly. The Holy Spirit is the animator of the mission.

So simple. So clear. So freeing.

I rise immediately from my prayer space, step into my office, fire up the laptop and printer, and produce a sign that reads: *Open for business! Under new management!*

I return to my prayer space feeling joyful, feeling free to forge ahead with the work that gives me life.

I am speaking here of prayer which is a way of being in relationship with God, not only during those intentional times of prayer, but in all times, in all things. And in surprising and unpredicted ways.

Prayer, I discover, encompasses the whole of my life, because this is the way God does relationship.

Yet prayer is more. Prayer, I discover, also is a form of waking up.

Prayer: Waking up to Jesus' conversation with his Father

I am speaking here of an interior waking up, which is a necessary work of the maturing life. Certainly of the maturing Christian life.

Waking up to what a life lived in God actually looks like,. Waking up to what prayer looks like in one who willingly embraces the radical poverty and contingency of life as necessary conditions for entry into God.

In his ragged-edged humanity, Jesus shows me what it means to lean into God as though my life depends on it. Because my life, like his, does in fact depend on it. My life depends on the leaning in, on the willingness to trust.

This leaning into God is the leaning of faith. Not leaning into God as a concept. Not God as benevolent rescuer.

I am speaking of actually leaning into God who is Soul of my soul, Breath of my breath, Flesh and Blood of my own flesh and blood.

So the conversation of Jesus with his Father, in part, is about words, some of which are captured in the Gospels. But the heart of this conversation is the relationship itself. The leaning in. The eternal gaze of love, which Rublev's icon of Holy Trinity reveals: eternal Real Presence.

"The Father and I are one," Jesus tells his disciples. "To see me is to see the Father."

And then he adds: *"Do you believe this?"* (see John 14:7-10).

Prayer, in part, is a waking up to Jesus' complete identification with his Father, and therefore a waking up to the intimacy and trust and freedom and joy embedded in such prayer. A waking up to the intimacy and trust and freedom and joy which is mine, too, when I truly am in Christ and Christ truly is in me.

I think of Jesus praying to his Father when he is healing the man who is deaf and unable to speak. Jesus "emits a groan," Saint Mark records (see Mark 7:31-37).

And when Jesus comes to the place where his friend Lazarus is buried, he groans twice, so deeply troubled in spirit is he, with the groanings of the Holy Spirit, groanings too deep for words. Groanings which rise as prayer from the gut.

We pray this groaning prayer too, especially when we hear of tragedy, or come upon the scene of grief unfolding. In these groaning prayers the soul instinctively knows that words cannot touch the intensity of the moment. The preverbal part of the self simply intercedes. The Holy Spirit shapes and carries the prayer.

Jesus' spirit also leaps up in praise to his Father, proclaiming that what is hidden from "the wise and learned ones" has been revealed to the merest children.

In fact, a childlike spirit is necessary, Jesus insists, to gain entry into the reign of God (see Matthew 18:1-5).

Jesus prays to his Father as he undergoes the most anguished testing of his vocation, in his agony in the garden of Gethsemane. "Father," he cries, "take this cup away from me. But, not my willing but yours."

All three synoptic Gospels—of Mark, Matthew, and Luke—record these words, suggesting that early church held this anguished prayer of the Lord as encouragement for its own time of persecution for its faith in the One who suffered death by crucifixion and was raised from the dead.

And finally, we hear Jesus pray to his Father in his final hours. Helplessly suspended between heaven and earth, Jesus cries out lines from the Psalms, the anguished soul still driven to communicate.

"My God, my God, why have you forsaken me?" he prays, lines from Psalm 22, the anguished prayer of an innocent person whose only recourse is God.

And again, Jesus cries out, "Father, into your hands I commend my spirit," lines from Psalm 31, a prayer in time of distress. Yet a prayer also which concludes in blessing God for deliverance.

I think about how impoverished my prayer would be, how impoverished my efforts to move with integrity and trust through my own times of testing, if I could not hear Jesus' prayer in his own times of testing.

Sobered, I sit with these words of Jesus praying to his Father, because I know that these words apprentice me, even now, to the times when I will undergo anguish and the temptation to flee.

What will I cry out in my hour of severe testing, I wonder. What will you cry out?

A story of prayer in a time of anguish

I am maybe eleven or so. My younger brothers are maybe eight and seven. Mother is driving us, after school, up into the forested West Hills of Portland, up Terwilliger Road, to the V.A. hospital.

Daddy has undergone a terribly painful test today, and we are going to visit him.

Actually, I have overheard what this test is. And all day long, as I sit through one class and then another, all I can think about is what my Daddy is going through today, the suffering. I think about what they are doing to him, and how terribly alone he must feel while I sit in class. I try hard to hold in all this anguish.

What the doctors are doing to my Daddy is injecting dye into his spinal fluid so that they can take an x-ray of his brain to see just where the tumor is, and to determine whether they can remove it.

"This test is excruciatingly painful," Mother tells me.

Silently I imagine the spinal fluid, the dye, the dye now moving into the brain, my Daddy's brain. And I try hard to hold it all together.

We arrive at the hospital, a cold monstrosity of a building. And by sheer will I put one foot in front of the other, trying to act normal, fighting back the tears that press hard behind my eyeballs. Trying to walk as though I were walking, perhaps, down a hallway at school.

My knees, my legs, my gut and heart all grip tight against the moment. Instinctively I learn what "solemn" means. I am feeling solemn right now.

We walk down the corridor to Daddy's ward, and enter the large room. I look over to his bed. He is not there.

"Oh, Pat's not back yet from that test," one of his ward mates says as soon as we enter. I feel a somber mood in the room.

"That's a terrible test," another one says. "We all knew when the dye hit the brain, because down these two long corridors, through two sets of closed metal doors, we could hear Pat crying out the words of the Hail Mary."

Inside I double over with anguish.

I know the words of the Hail Mary. Right now they stab my heart with their urgency and beauty. And through a dense, dark, interior fog of pain I am consoled, knowing that these words were my Daddy's consolation, his shelter, as he lay pinned down against the needle.

So this is no idle question that I sit with: What will I cry out in my hour of extreme anguish?

What will you cry out?

Another story: Receiving a spirit of faithfulness, of peace

I am maybe twelve or so. Old enough to begin to appreciate what my father is about.

He is a man of quiet suffering, living as he does with an inoperable brain tumor. A barber, a humble man, supporting his family of six.

And he is a holy man.

And so I am quietly pleased that my place, in the pew on Sunday mornings, is next to him.

I watch him, from a sideways glance, as he sits quietly in these ten minutes before Mass starts. He is reading the lives of the saints whose feast days will be celebrated in the coming week. He prays the prayers before Mass. He readies himself for communion.

He is a man whose soul is deeply at peace.

He is at peace with his life, and with his fate, and with his God. Sitting silently, he is my teacher. My spiritual teacher.

As we sit side by side, I am aware that my upper arm rests ever so gently against his upper arm. And the peace within his soul flows like the sweetest balm into my soul.

Sunday after Sunday I undergo my spiritual formation.

Essentials of prayer: Humility, poverty of spirit, trust

I am convinced that humility—not need but humility—is the foundation of prayer.

God knows what I need, what I care about deeply, and what requires divine attention in addition to my own.

In fact, Jesus says as much: Your heavenly Father knows all the things that you need.

As though my reciting my list of concerns might inform God of something new, or draw God's attention to something unexplainably overlooked.

No, the first essential element of prayer is humility.

Real humility is actually a genuine honesty. Humility means knowing, and honestly admitting, who I am before God.

Sinner? Yes. Incomplete? Absolutely. Striving and oftentimes sorely missing the mark? Oh, yes.

Yet in real humility I also must be genuinely honest, knowing also that who I am before God is Beloved, anointed richly and decisively in the Holy Spirit. That I walk around with the flesh of pure Mystery, flesh of the risen Christ, embedded within my flesh, the blood of the risen Christ flowing in my veins.

To knowledge this astonishing truth of my being also is an expression of real humility.

Such humility is the living expression of what Saint Paul describes as "the weight of glory" (see 2 Corinthians 4:17).

"Humility" suggests, poetically, *humus,* that slimy substance that results from the decaying process of plant and animal matter. The stuff of the soil of Earth.

The person of genuine humility is lowly in a way that nourishes life, just as humus nourishes garden beds or the forest floor. Joyful humility, Saint Francis of Assisi shows time and time again, enriches others, blesses others.

Humility joyfully recognizes that "apart from God, I am nothing." As Isaiah declares: "It is God who has accomplished all we have done" (see Isaiah 26:12).

Jesus values humility as the preeminent virtue of right relationship in the reign of God. "Those who humble themselves like a child," he teaches, "will be greatest in the kingdom of heaven" (see Matthew 18:4).

And again: "If you exalt yourself, you will be humbled. But, if you humble yourself, you will be exalted" (see Matthew 23:12).

Saint Paul describes this virtue of humility in Jesus in this way:

> Though he was in the form of God,
> Jesus did not deem equality with God as
> something to be grasped. (see Philippians 2:6)

Jesus describes himself as "meek and humble of heart" (see Matthew 11:28-30). God can work with this quality of spirit. Jesus is pliant, shapeable, conformable to the Father's willing. Not because it is easy, but because it is exquisitely perfect, and therefore beautiful.

Humility allows me—invites me, impels me, really—to put my forehead down on my prayer table each morning and say what I know to be most true: "Your servant, Lord, your servant am I." I understand clearly the right ordering within the relationship.

This, too, is exquisitely perfect, and therefore beautiful.

Humility is countercultural. Or let me say, it is not the norm. When someone in the public spotlight—a sports figure, a cultural icon, a politician, a religious leader—expresses genuine humility, we take note.

Given this virtue's prominence in the actions of the very visible Pope Francis, genuine humility stands a chance of "trending." Genuine humility, clothed in genuine joy, is disarmingly attractive to the human spirit.

Genuine humility, clothed in genuine joy, reveals the reign of God. In fact, it reveals *God*.

The prophet Micah reminds the people of God of what they are to do: "Only to do the right and to love goodness, / and to walk humbly with your God" (Micah 6:8).

If the line were to read "walk quickly with your God" I would assume that God is walking quickly. Or if it were to read "walk smartly with your God," I would assume that God is walking smartly.

But the passage reads "walk humbly with your God." Which tells me that God walks humbly. And the only way that I can walk in God's company is to walk humbly, too.

The second essential element of prayer, poverty of spirit, or what I call gospel poverty, walks hand-in-hand with humility. It is first an attitude, an interior disposition, which forms the proper posture for prayer.

Poverty of spirit is the first of the beatitudes, preeminent among the blessings of a life lived in service to the reign of God.

When I am "poor in spirit" I am free to acknowledge what is inescapably true of my life: I am radically dependent on God for everything—from heartbeat and breath to fruitfulness in my labors.

Poverty of spirit is not destitution, but rather an openness to God's unbidden generosity, so that I, in turn, can bless others with that same generosity. A poverty, the Apostle Paul writes, which enriches others.

I find something very here-and-now in this element of prayer, poverty of spirit. Queen Esther, "seized with mortal fear," cries out to God, "I am utterly alone. I have no help but you" (see Esther C:12-14).

My admission of radical dependence on God sets God free, so to speak, to animate the good I seek. This poverty of spirit frees me, in my prayer, from having to prove my worthiness or justify myself before God. And therefore, poverty of spirit frees me to receive what God most desires to give me.

Jesus points to this essential aspect of prayer when he warns against "praying like the hypocrites" who love to be noticed for their piety. Rather, he says, "go to your inner room, close the door, and pray to your Father in secret" (Matthew 6:6).

Poverty of spirit allows for the honest conversation which leads to real prayer. So real, I discover, that I am changed from the inside out.

The third essential element of prayer is trust. If trust were a gesture, it would be hands opening, from white-knuckle grip of what most worries me, to hands wide open, palms extended upward.

If trust were an action, it would be the careful and loving work of placing upon the altar what I most urgently pray for. Placing upon the altar and not snatching back. Placing, and then gently, reverently, trustingly, walking away.

In the biblical understanding, once I place something upon the alar of sacrifice, I cannot take it back. It is no longer mine. It now is offered.

Likewise, the matter of my prayer now is no longer in my hands but in God's hands.

This is what trust means: Saying what needs to be said, opening my heart so that everything within it can spill out, placing it all upon the altar of sacrifice, and then stepping away, so that God can be, well, GOD.

As soon as I snatch from the altar what I have heartfully placed there, I have in essence said to God: I believe in You. I trust You. But in this matter, *You are not enough.* I need to clutch this matter some more. I am not ready to release it to You.

This snatching back and clutching, whether in prayer or in relationships, is called "worry." And worry is spiritually, emotionally, and relationally toxic.

We live in a culture that is deep in the grip of worry.

Worry sells. Worry about anything. Worry about everything. Worry to the point of interior paralysis.

For some people, worry is an expression of "love." The logic goes like this: If I worry constantly about you, especially in my prayer, you will know how much I love you, and how very much I care about you.

Worry in personal relationships easily becomes, knowingly or not, a means of coercion through guilt.

Jesus has a blunt word for people who carry worry into prayer. He admonishes: "Stop thinking like a pagan!" (see Matthew 6:25-34).

Worry does not trust the logic of grace. It shuts out the sheer delight of grace, the subtle and utterly transformative work of grace.

Trust—quite the opposite of worry—leans into grace, anticipates grace, makes room for grace. Trust, in prayer, defends a space for the deep work of grace to actually yield results.

Trust is not something I feel when I am in charge and things are going my way. Trust is the act of "leaning in" to God when I acknowledge that I am not in charge but that God is in charge, and I am OK with that.

When I get myself and my worries out of the way, things become free to go God's way.

My capacity for trust changes how I pray.

My capacity for trust, therefore, changes how I actually reveal God to others, how I reveal the risen Christ. Maybe in words, but surely in the joyful generosity and freedom with which I live.

In short, a maturing capacity for trust changes how I evangelize.

So, how do I enter into a meaningful reflection on my life that will deepen the conversation of my prayer?

Five questions to deepen the conversation of prayer

Nothing in my life, nor in yours, lies outside the realm of God's compassion and mercy. The concerns of your heart and mine are God's concerns first, and therefore our hearts are moved to feel as God feels, and, with grace, to respond as we imagine God would respond.

Which means: Your experience matters to God. My experience matters to God. And the experience of those whom I think could do better, the experience of those who backslide because they have lost their grip on hope, the experience of those who make choices that I would never make—their experience also matters to God.

To paraphrase Saint Paul: God rejoices with those who rejoice, and weeps with those who weep (see Romans 12:15). Nothing falls outside the embrace of God's compassion and care.

I discover that not only my experience but the quality of my life and how I reflect on it matters to God. The quality of my life is shaped by the values I not merely profess but actually live.

If compassion is a value, my life will be shaped by deeds and expressions of compassion. If trust is a value, my life will be shaped by courageous actions that make sense only because God exists.

Equally, how I reflect on my life—on my experiences and the quality of my life—matters to God.

Reflection, guided by the Holy Spirit, becomes an opening to grace. When I reflect on God's movement in my life, and the patterns of this movement, I open up a space both for my prayer and for God's desiring to bear fruit in my life and in the lives of those I will touch.

My reflection begins, often, with naming things.

The simple work of naming things gives me a way to get close to what is real, close to what I most need to notice. Five simple questions lead me to the heart of my lived experience, and therefore they give me the simple, honest words I most need to bring to the conversation of my prayer.

First, what gives me joy?

It may help to describe this word "joy."

I experience joy as an interior stirring of the Holy Spirit when my life, my actions, touch others in a way that blesses them.

Applying myself to the work for which I am gifted, or uplifting a friend, making space for a stranger, or creative engagement that benefits others, or compassionate engagement that relieves the distress of others —all of these activities are examples, for me, of the experience of joy.

Joy is a sure sign of the Holy Spirit at work. It is a preeminent fruit of the Holy Spirit in the maturing Christ-centered life. The joy which I experience is a participation in God's joy.

Joy always moves outward, always blesses others in some way. Joy, therefore, is a reliable indicator of mission.

It is important that I be able to notice and name what gives me joy, so that I can notice and name my mission as it matures.

Second, what robs me of joy?

What robs me of joy in this season of my life may be what gave me joy in an earlier season: an assignment that now is over, perhaps, which I have not let go.

Or what robs me of joy may be my resistance to an invitation to grow in new ways, preferring instead to dig in my heels.

What robs me of joy may be old wounds, unforgiveness, or old hurtful messages that continue to play in an endless loop in my memory.

What robs me of joy may be relationships or activities or habits, or even addictions, that stand in the way of deeper engagement in my mission.

Or what robs me of joy may be a pervasive sense of being vocationally or relationally or existentially lost.

But until I can name what robs me of joy, I cannot maintain, or reclaim, vocational and missional clarity. Because God's answer to my prayer, "Dear God, what do you want me to do," will always be: "Do what gives you joy, and that blesses others."

Third, what breaks my heart?

How easily I become numb to the daily newsfeed of human greed, human suffering, and the massive loss of hope in my twenty-first century world.

Necessary for heartbreak, which is part of the maturing human experience, is a life lived in a way, and at a pace, which allows for love, for human connection and compassion, for engagement in life beyond the borders of my home.

I can avoid heartbreak by structuring my life so that what is most human, and therefore most vulnerable and complex and messy, can never find a way into my schedule.

Yet if I am an apostle of the Lord, certain things will break my heart and spur me to action, to moral action. Certain things will break my heart because they first break the heart of God.

The heart sealed against heartbreak is a heart sealed against grace.

To defend my own humanity, and the humanity of others, I need to be conscious of, and able to name, what breaks my heart.

Fourth, what am I resisting?

The quality of my life—as a maturing human being and as one who is anointed in the Holy Spirit—depends on my openness to God's invitations.

I am convinced that God is All Invitation. So my openness—or resistance—to God's invitations determines whether God's invitations will bear fruit in my life, especially for the good of others.

I can run with the grace, or I can stubbornly insist on trying to go forward with the brakes on. I can—and sometimes do—resist opportunities to grow toward my fuller self-in-God.

I can run, but ultimately I cannot hide, from the One who is passionate about my life, my joy, my fruitfulness; passionate about calling forth the dignity and inherent beauty of my maturing, ever-evolving personhood.

In fact, I can exhaust myself in my resistance to grace. But why would I want to resist grace?

Fifth, what am I accepting?

Accepting, or resisting, the unbidden invitations of the maturing anointed life has everything to do with mission, with missional fruitfulness—or not.

What I am accepting may be that I always was and always will be a good B-plus student. That I will never be as polished, or witty, or as acclaimed, as the person I think I should be.

Or, I may be accepting the reality that I am richly anointed to accomplish certain good for these few people whose lives I will touch in the course of my brief journey.

Or, I may be accepting other limitations, other poverties, which may seem inherently unfair: a poverty of health or mobility, a poverty of education or experience, a poverty of connections, or friendships, or love.

When I accept my conditions—whether undesired poverties or unbidden riches—the mere act of acceptance gives God something to work with.

The quality of my life and the way I reflect on it indeed matters as I mature in life. "Come, let us sit in counsel together," the Lord God urges (see Isaiah 45:21).

This is the same Lord God who walks humbly, so that I might learn how to walk humbly, too, with God hidden beside me, and in me, as I walk through my twenty-first century world.

A closing story: "My inner name is Joy"

It is a foggy, damp, pearl-gray morning here in San Francisco, where I stand at the corner of Fillmore and Bush Streets, waiting for the light to change. At age twenty-five I am achingly aware that I have no impelling vision for my life.

Interiorly I feel the dense gray fog which has settled in, a blanket of nagging depression which I cannot seem to shake. I have no idea where my life is going.

Little do I know, at twenty-five, that this blanket of nagging depression will hang over me another twenty years. Sometimes lifting for a season, sometimes looking as though it might dissipate. But never really going away.

Even as I stand here at the street corner, it is not lost on me that I am in many ways, especially interiorly, waiting for the light to change.

And though no ray of light has broken through the dense morning fog, an interior beam of light unexpectedly breaks through my soul.

"My inner name is Joy," I clearly hear.

My inner name is Joy.

This is odd, I think. No one in my family is named Joy. Joy is not a name I connect with.

And in the same instant I understand clearly that I will not be able to touch or to experience this joy now.

Still, I know with absolute certainty that this inner name has been given to me. Pure gift, revealed to me, in a promissory way.

Equally in the same instant I receive the assurance: *No one can take this joy from me.*

The traffic light changes. I cross the street and continue on my mile-long walk to morning Mass, carrying what is sure but hidden, hidden even from me. Held in trust, deep within me.

With Sarah of the Genesis scripture, I can say: "The one who makes the promise is worthy of the trust" (see Hebrews 11:11, referring to Genesis 17:15-19).

Joy. Untouchable, yet fully pledged.

QUESTIONS FOR REFLECTION, JOURNALING,
OR CONVERSATION

Looking back

What insights into "prayer as holy conversation" have been most meaningful for me? Which phrases speak to me? Which images?

What experiences of "prayer as holy conversation" in my own life come to mind—from my earlier years? from the middle span of time? or from the present or recent past?

How might the Lord be apprenticing me in the ways of prayer as holy conversation? How would I describe this apprenticeship?

Looking forward

How might I apply these insights into prayer, to more deeply form my own prayer practices?

What word, or phrase, or insight, seems to be the gift that will carry me forward?

The prayer that comes to me now …

PART 3

PRAYER AS INVITATION TO SOMETHING MORE
A retreat in three movements

We have journeyed together into prayer as encounter, and prayer as holy conversation.

Now we journey into prayer as invitation—specifically, invitation to "something more."

I am speaking of the invitation to something that will stretch you, strengthen you, challenge you, and fulfill you in the unique assignment which is *your* life, and no one else's.

My own journeying has taught me a certain truth: At some point in our lives, each of us must enter, and will enter, into the one encounter that will radically shape us and define us as the uniquely lovable and loving and fruitful person we always were meant to be.

At some point we each are called forth in a way that will override our resistances to grace and to the good which we believed we were not worthy to receive.

Which means that at some point we must courageously engage
ourselves in the one holy conversation that will call us forth, in the power
of our anointing, and set us free.

At some point in our lives we must actually accept the invitation we
have longed for our entire life, whether we have known it or named it or
owned it—or not.

I am speaking of the invitation which we could not have imagined, or
summoned up, were we left to our own devices.

And I am speaking here of the divine invitation to something more,
which is utterly unique to your personhood and to your mission in this
life.

I am speaking of the defining invitation which sets you free to give
yourself wholeheartedly to the worthy relationship and the noble work by
which you will bless others.

A word about this "something more"

The "something more" which you may have in mind for your life
may be a faint glimpse, a mere wisp of an intuition, into what God has in
mind for your life.

And when you move toward this glimpse or intuition, or begin to
move with it, you give God something to work with.

Experience tells me that the "something more" which God desires to
give you is actually life in Christ Jesus.

I mean a life, lived wholeheartedly, transparently, that eventually
utterly disappears in Christ Jesus. Yes, disappears into Jesus of the

Gospels, who lived and taught and healed and prayed, and who refused to let anything come between him and his mission to reveal the reign of God.

I mean also a life that, eventually, utterly disappears in Christ Jesus—whom the Gospels proclaim was anointed, sent, sorely resisted, challenged, arrested, tortured, crucified, buried, and raised from the dead.

I mean a life hidden in the One with the nail scars, with the scar, too, of a life-draining lance wound in his side, who now lives.

The "something more" that you are invited to experience is a life, lived now—perhaps haltingly, sometimes distractedly—yet a life already being transformed, purified, and ever more deeply anointed in the Spirit of the risen Christ.

This "something more" is a life that celebrates the good, honors the losses, embraces the complexities, and lives at peace with the questions.

The "something more" to which you are invited is nothing short of a life in which you can say, in joy and humility, with the Apostle Paul: "I live now, no longer I but Christ lives in me" (see Galatians 2:20).

Complete transformation in Christ risen. This is the larger invitation which makes sense of all the smaller invitations. Complete transformation in Christ, precisely through all the obligations and urgencies, all the heartbreaks and hopes, of your particular life.

Complete transformation by love, into love. Into ... Love. Taking your rightful place at the banquet table of Holy Trinity, and entering now into the one heartbeat, the heartbeat of God.

A word about "invitation"

I regard the word "invitation" as a rich spiritual word.

I have discovered, in my life, that I actually am not the initiator of anything. All is invitation, and all is grace.

When I get an idea to do something, or to say or to write something, or to undertake some courageous new adventure, I may think that I am the initiator. But I am not the initiator.

I am invited.

The very idea to act in some way, or to say or do something, is sheer grace, the hidden movement of the Holy Spirit. The idea to act is, in truth, the invitation. It comes unexpected, untamed, unrehearsed, a hunch or intuition that interrupts the ordinary.

The mere notion to act in some way or to say or do something is a visitation of grace.

These larger, irresistible, defining invitations will never be merely to "more of the same."

They may be the opening to yet deeper engagement in what you already do, or the opening to a yet more mature commitment to relationships of importance, or to the work or way of life that already engages you.

Or, the invitation may take you off your familiar path, or away from the life in which you have grown comfortable. But the invitation will not pull you off mission or away from your anointing to live deeply in Christ.

The invitation may startle you. It may seriously capture your attention, as did the messenger Gabriel's startling irruption into the life of a young girl in the Galilean backwater town of Nazareth.

Or, the invitation may come like sweet late-harvest fruit after a season of hard work, a season of faithfulness and trust. The invitation may come after a season of waiting for what you could not exactly name, but whose promise swelled your heart each time you pondered it.

I have learned that I cannot craft the invitation. I cannot make the invitation happen. I cannot hurry it. I cannot demand it. I can only hold open a pure and hopeful space where the invitation may enter.

My work in the meantime is to live faithfully, and wholeheartedly, here and now, tending to the demands of what is before me, so that when the time of invitation arrives, I will be ready.

I cannot rush through the season of waiting. But I am free to ask the Lord in prayer: "Might you have an invitation for me? An invitation to something more?"

And I imagine the Lord instantly filled with joy at the question, unable to resist such readiness and trust.

This question, "Might you have an invitation for me," is a spiritual question, indeed a holy question, because it sets the Holy Spirit free to be the active agent in my life.

This question, "Might you have an invitation for me," is radically different from the question, "Lord Jesus, what do you want me to do?" Or worse, the statement usually uttered in exhaustion, "I don't *know* what you want me to do."

These two prayers are guaranteed to go *clunk* on the floor of heaven.

The first question, "What do you want me to do," begs for an opening up of holy imagination which comes from the practice of noticing things.

The second statement, "I don't know what you want me to do," is the consequence of exhaustion, a frustration that affirms that I have been pushing against the flow of grace.

These two prayers fail to open space for the creative work of the Holy Spirit. And therefore they have no place in the anointed life of an apostle of the Lord.

The question, "Might you have an invitation for me," communicates to me as much as to the Lord that I am available, open to divine possibility, quite agreeable, even, to what God might have in mind, even though I may have no idea right now what these words mean.

As you prepare for this retreat in three movements, take time right now to place yourself in the presence of the Lord. He has invited you to this moment. And he is inviting you now to journey with him, and to journey into him, into life in God.

PRAYER AS INVITATION TO SOMETHING MORE
A retreat in three movements

For this self-paced retreat you will need a restful, uninterrupted space. This is not a "retreat on the run" but a time consecrated, set aside for a holy purpose.

This restful, uninterrupted space may be a quiet room in your living quarters, or it may be a chapel, or a quiet room in a nearby monastery.

"Quiet" includes no distractions from electronic devices, or from family members or work commitments that promise to fall apart in your absence. You might even consider leaving your electronic devices and other means of connection behind.

In other words, in this retreat time make it easy for "heart to speak to heart."

And you will need some way to capture ideas. This may be a journal, or simply ruled or blank pages. Or, if you prefer artistic expression, have your art supplies at the ready.

Feel free to write out your thoughts in each portion of the retreat, not just in the "Journaling" portion.

If your way of capturing ideas is by using an electronic device, you will need to exercise discipline in not "checking in" or "messaging out" during your retreat time.

And bring your bible.

If your only bible is in an app on your phone, I encourage you to invest in a real printed bible. Or borrow a bible. This journey into Scripture is not a "scan and scroll" experience but an invitation to sit deeply with the Word, in its rich visual and tactile context.

My well-used bible, with dog-eared pages and underlined and highlighted text, with notes wedged into the margins, is a cherished spiritual companion to me in ways that an app on my phone can never be.

This retreat in three movements focuses on:
"Prayer as encounter," drawing from John 20:11-16a: *"Who are you looking for?"*
"Prayer as holy conversation," drawing from Luke 6:12-13: *He spent the night in communion with God*
"Prayer as invitation to something more," drawing from Matthew 14:22-29: *And Jesus said, "Come!"*

Each movement will walk you through:
The reading
The sitting
Reflection questions
Conversation with Jesus
The journaling
A closing prayer

Movement 1: Prayer as Encounter

Opening Scripture
    John 20:11-16a
    "Who are you looking for?"

The reading

Please read this passage aloud, in a gentle voice. Invite the reading to be prayerful for you.

Let the words, the scene, the tone, the images find a place to settle in.

Rest with the passage. Savor it. Take your time with this first reading of the text.

The sitting

Now, pray the passage aloud, unrushed, a second time.

In this second reading, do you notice a change in your voice? Do the words seem to come from a deeper, quieter place within?

If necessary, read the passage a third time to allow it to shift interiorly to a place of deeper resonance.

With a few deep, intentional breaths, expand the walls of your heart, your mind, your imagination. Let the words, the images, the actions and interactions invite you deeper into the scene.

Silently sit with the text. Savor it. Notice what words or actions or images come forward to be savored.

Take as long as you wish with this sitting. This is your time with the Lord. He has been waiting, and longing, for this cherished time with you.

Reflection questions on "prayer as encounter"

Ask yourself these questions, and capture your ideas in the ways that work best for you.

Have I ever wept deeply over the loss of a loved one? Wept at the funeral, or at the burial site, when the loss was still fresh, still raw?

Or, have I ever wept deeply over a loved one who has walked away—from me? from family? from church? from Christian faith?

Who was this loved one? Who was this loved one *to me?* And what was this experience of deep grieving like for me?

Have I searched in a crowd, hoping to find my loved one again? Or yearned to hold this loved one just one more time? To say the words I had meant to say? Or perhaps the words that come now, only in the loss?

Do I hold the beautiful question that would invite worthy conversation that might bring back the loved one who has walked away?

What is this experience of searching and longing like for me?

In my deepest grief and loneliness, has anyone—a friend, a stranger, "the gardener"—spoken my name, called me forth, and helped me to feel whole, and valued, and loved? What was this experience of being called forth in love like for me?

Conversation with Jesus

Lord Jesus, the Gospels reveal, in so many instances, that to know you is to know you in relationship with your Father.

Can I say also, of myself, that to know me is to know me in relationship with you? This is the way I desire to be known, as one who lives in relationship with you.

Might you be asking me, in my own life now, "Who *are* you looking for," just as you asked your cherished disciple Mary of Magdala?

Where am I, in my life now, that might cause me to feel that I cannot find you? How would I describe where I am in relation to you? Have you drifted away? Or, have I drifted?

Who *am* I actually looking for? I want to say that I am looking for you. That I am like the deer thirsting for running streams.

Yet what if, in my own life, you are cleverly disguised as someone I take for granted, someone I dismiss as "just the gardener."

Are you asking me, perhaps even daily, perhaps especially in my restless and unfulfilled moments, "Who *are* you looking for? Who, really, are you looking for?"

And what might I say in reply?

In my day-to-day life, what am I actually looking for? What do I keep expecting? An encounter with you? A sense of purpose? A way to be helpful? The next assignment?

Am I looking for distractions from what I do not want to face? A way to relieve the pain of loneliness? or of lostness? A way to relieve the pain of irrelevance? or perhaps failure?

What am I actually looking for? How shall I describe it? Lord Jesus, how shall *we* describe it?

The journaling

Lord Jesus, these are my thoughts as we enter, together, more deeply into conversation on "my prayer as encounter …"

(Allow the Holy Spirit as much unrushed time as needed.)

A closing prayer

Lord Jesus, I deeply desire that "to know me" is to know me in relationship with you.

I desire that my prayer might be not just words spoken into the abyss but a real encounter, with you, Jesus, crucified Lord and risen Christ.

I desire to encounter you, who are present to me, now. You beholding me as cherished disciple, fully anointed for apostleship, and invited by you into friendship.

Lord Jesus, I desire to encounter you in my life, where I am right now.

And I desire to encounter you, also, where *you* are, as you invite me to go beyond myself, beyond the safe and the known.

I desire to encounter you as you invite me, now, into my fullest self-in-you.

Receive, Lord Jesus, this prayer of my heart.

Amen.

MOVEMENT 2: PRAYER AS HOLY CONVERSATION

Opening Scripture
    Luke 6:12-13
    He spent the night in communion with God.

The reading

    Please read this passage aloud, in a gentle voice. Invite the reading to be prayerful for you.

    Let the words, the scene, the tone, the images find a place to settle in.

    Rest with the passage. Savor it. Take your time with this first reading of the text.

The sitting

    Now, pray the passage aloud, unrushed, a second time.

    In this second reading, do you notice a change in your voice? Do the words seem to come from a deeper, quieter place within?

    If necessary, read the passage a third time to allow it to shift interiorly to a place of deeper resonance.

    With a few deep, intentional breaths, expand the walls of your heart, your mind, your imagination. Let the words, the images, the actions and interactions invite you deeper into the scene.

Silently sit with the text. Savor it. Notice what words or actions or images come forward to be savored.

Take as long as you wish with this sitting. This is your time with the Lord. He has been waiting, and longing, for this cherished time with you.

Reflection questions on "prayer as holy conversation"

Ask yourself these questions, and capture your ideas in the ways that work best for you.

When I pray, where do I go?

Not where I think about going, or hope someday to go. But where do I actually go, to get away from the crush of life, in order to pray?

When I am in this place of prayer, what is this experience like for me?

Or, if my deepest prayer is *in* the crush of life—perhaps like the medic on the battlefield—what is this experience of prayer like for me?

When I imagine Jesus spending the night "in communion with God," what might that experience have been like for him?

Do I ever feel inclined to pray, or feel urgently drawn to pray, in the late night or early morning hours?

When I am in prayer, how do I actually enter into "communion with God"? If I have never experienced this type of prayer, what do I imagine such an encounter to be like?

On a daily basis, where do I go to "put my heart with the heart of God"? What do I actually do to "put my desiring with God's desiring"?

Is my prayer consistent? Is it intentional? Does my prayer reflect the maturity of my years? Does it reflect my responsibilities?

When I have prepared for major life commitments—marriage, schooling, a career, or career change, or other major commitment—how have I brought these commitments to prayer?

Did this prayer feel like "holy conversation"?

Currently, in my life choices, is my prayer in times of discernment more intimate, more trusting, more an engagement in "holy conversation" than it may have been in the past?

Conversation with Jesus

Lord Jesus, as you began to discern and grow into the magnitude of your mission, perhaps you sensed that you needed to draw others into your work of revealing the reign of God. Perhaps you knew that you could not go into this mission alone.

Perhaps you understood that this mission had to be shared with others, entrusted to them. That it could never be just about you.

You did not call forth everyone who followed you. You called forth a few. And they in turn would call forth others.

The scriptures tell us that before you called forth these few, you spent the night in deep prayer. You put your heart with the heart of your Father, so important was this next step in your mission.

You were about to entrust your mission to an unlikely band of disciples. Some of them laborers. Some young and dreamy. One, in the end, would betray you for cash.

Still, you trusted, and prayed, and kept your heart with the heart of your Father.

Like you, I have taken important next steps in my own mission.

And as I give myself more fully to you, I will take many more "important next steps," each calling forth from me everything I am, everything I have. Each step demanding courage and complete trust in you.

Apprentice me, Lord Jesus, as you apprenticed your early followers.

Apprentice me in the ways of prayer.

You show me how prayer is done: by stepping away to a place removed, a "mountain wilderness." Not in the comfort of home but where the soul is free to encounter its poverty, its precarity, its utter dependence on God, and the wild freedom which this dependence brings.

Apprentice me to the disciplines of prayer, to the work of leaning deep into God, not in order to decide my next steps, but to receive from God the invitation to confidently take the next step, and then the next, even when I cannot see the path.

Apprentice me, Lord Jesus, to the night of prayer, and to the day of action. Apprentice me to the holy freedom which is mine, because I am yours.

Conform my heart, and my desiring, to your heart, and to your desiring, so that prayer as communion with God will be, for me, the norm, as it was for you.

So conform me to yourself that every conversation I have with others will flow from the one holy conversation at the core of my soul.

The journaling

Lord Jesus, these are my thoughts as we enter, together, more deeply into this "prayer as holy conversation with God ..."

(Allow the Holy Spirit as much unrushed time as needed.)

A closing prayer

Lord Jesus, the deepest part of me yearns to be "in communion with God."

I know that this is not really my yearning. It is the yearning of the Holy Spirit within me.

And so I expect that this yearning for communion with God will change me.

And I expect that this holy conversation, of my heart with the heart of God, will change me. This divine indwelling, this *communio.*

And more, I expect that this holy conversation will change others who encounter me, because this holy conversation, this divine indwelling, will shape my ways of being in the world.

And now I dare to ask the courageous question.

Where, and how, and when, Lord Jesus, do you desire to "spend the night in communion with God" through me?

Is it tonight? Is it an early rising tomorrow? Or perhaps one day soon?

You lead the way. I will go where you lead, to allow you this intimate conversation with your Father, through me.

I know already, by the way my heart stirs, that our time together in prayer will not be an inconvenience to me but a path of joy and an experience of peace.

Let me be the temple in which you praise and worship and beseech and adore your Father, Lord Jesus, in the quiet spaces.

Amen.

MOVEMENT 3: PRAYER AS INVITATION TO SOMETHING MORE

Opening Scripture
 Matthew 14:22-29
 And Jesus said, "Come!"

The reading

Please read this passage aloud, in a gentle voice. Invite the reading to be prayerful for you.

Let the words, the scene, the tone, the images find a place to settle in.

Rest with the passage. Savor it. Take your time with this first reading of the text.

The sitting

Now, pray the passage aloud, unrushed, a second time.

In this second reading, do you notice a change in your voice? Do the words seem to come from a deeper, quieter place within?

If necessary, read the passage a third time to allow it to shift interiorly to a place of deeper resonance.

With a few deep, intentional breaths, expand the walls of your heart, your mind, your imagination. Let the words, the images, the actions and interactions invite you deeper into the scene.

Silently sit with the text. Savor it. Notice what words or actions or images come forward to be savored.

Take as long as you wish with this sitting. This is your time with the Lord. He has been waiting, and longing, for this cherished time with you.

Reflection questions on "prayer as invitation to something more"

Ask yourself these questions, and capture your ideas in the ways that work best for you.

In this passage, Jesus again goes up on the mountain, alone, to pray into the night. He seems so deeply absorbed in the conversation that he transcends the laws of physics. He walks on the sea.

When I pray, do I ever feel so absorbed in God that I seem to transcend time and space, as Jesus did? How would I describe this experience of being deeply absorbed in prayer?

When does this quality of prayer occur for me? During certain forms of prayer? In certain places, or in certain circumstances of prayer?

Do I actively seek these deeply absorbing encounters with God in prayer?

What might hold me back from prayer that deeply absorbs me?

Like the disciples in the boat, what "storm," present or pending, might throw me into a state of fear?

As he did with Peter, how does Jesus call me out from my fear? How does he invite me, as he invited Peter, to transcend fear?

If fear is my hiding place, can I actually trust Jesus' invitation? Or is my fear greater than my ability to trust that he is Lord, and that he is actually calling me?

Like Peter, have I ever asked the Lord to command me to come to him across the uncertain surface of my own life? What were the circumstances? And what was this experience like for me?

Do I prefer to live my life on the uncertain surface, walking toward the One who calls me? Or do I prefer to live a predictable life in the relative security of the boat?

Either way, how would I describe this way of living? How does walking toward Jesus, or staying in the boat, render me effective in revealing the reign of God?

Conversation with Jesus

Lord Jesus, in this passage I find you apprenticing your disciples in an unlikely moment, in the midst of a storm, at night, out at sea.

This is not "classroom learning" but on-the-job apprenticeship.

On this night you apprentice your disciples to a transcendent life of radical trust and bold expectation.

Walking on water is not normal within the human experience. You know this well, Lord Jesus. Yet you, and Peter for a brief moment, do just this.

You never apprenticed your followers to the ways of magic, or to illusion of any sort. You apprenticed your followers to the ways of God. To ways that transcend the limits of logic and explanation.

Patiently, you apprenticed them. You showed them what radical trust in God, radical trust in you, actually looks like, and how it is actually done.

And now you apprentice me.

You show me that when I am in God, as you were in God, I should expect to do what Peter strived to do: to actually walk to you across the uncertain surface of my own time and circumstances.

Not because I have great powers, but because you have called me, and invited me to something far beyond my limitations.

And I discover that by the way I fix my eyes on you and walk toward you, one foot in front of the other, I affirm that you are fully worthy of my trust.

You offer me the freedom to let go all the "yes buts," all the hesitations. You offer me the freedom to let go my resistances and my excuses. You offer me the freedom to simply accept your invitation: *Come!*

You offer me this freedom now, as I sit here with you, in this moment.

With the full force of love you fix your eyes on me, hoping that I will fix my eyes on you in turn. You are hoping that I will fix my heart on yours, as your heart is fixed on mine.

My assignment is not to understand the logic, nor figure out the logistics.

My assignment, simply, is to take you at your word, to trust the invitation, to entrust the details to you, and to hoist myself out of my safe place and onto the only honest ground I have, which well may feel "uncertain."

In fact, it may feel terrifying.

You do not invite me to fall on my face. You invite me to trust you as Lord, and then to take the next courageous step.

Your only motive is love.

So simply is the power of God waiting to be revealed in me, and through my actions, my life.

You invite me to transcend my limitations, my failures, my resistances, my history. Always, you invite me to something more. And that something more is life lived fully, freely, generously, in you.

I want to live this life in you. I desire it. I want to be called out, called beyond myself, beyond my limitations, in order to live in you, and to reveal you at work in my life.

In fact, I ask you now, Master, to call me out. Call me beyond myself, beyond my limitations, so that I might reveal you everywhere.

The journaling

Lord Jesus, these are my thoughts as we enter, together, more deeply into conversation on "my prayer to invitation to something more ..."

(Allow the Holy Spirit as much unrushed time as needed.)

A closing prayer

Lord Jesus, my life is full of "uncertain surfaces," full of unknowns that threaten to trap me in the grip of fear. Sometimes I do feel like I am in a boat, in the night, unprotected, utterly at the mercies of a storm-tossed sea.

Perhaps I pray for your help and consolation. Perhaps I have a notion of what your help and consolation might look like, what your form of deliverance might be.

And when I do not experience the hope or consolation or deliverance which I have in mind, it is easy for me to grow discouraged, or to grow frightened, or angry, or lost.

Yet you never cease speaking to me the words I possibly do not want to hear: *Take courage, it is I; do not be afraid!*

You want to lift me out from my fears, certainly. Yet even more, you desire to call me forth, courageously, into my fully anointed self-in-God.

Come! you say to me.

I imagine you pleading with me: *Give me something to work with!*

Your invitation is so simple, so direct.

Come!

You have been speaking this one simple word of invitation all along, your eyes dancing with the joy of possibility as you behold the likes of me.

Do I take you at your word? Do I really want to live my life this unguardedly? this courageously?

Even now, in this moment, you issue the invitation again. It falls with great clarity upon my ears, my heart, as though for the first time.

Like Peter, I hoist one leg over the side of the boat. And now, with full intention, I hoist the other. I stand up straight. I turn toward you, and I fix my eyes on you. And I step free of the boat.

You bend your knees. I bend my knees. You spread your arms wide and throw back your head and roar in joyous laughter. I do the same.

I am starting to get the feel of real freedom. Freedom in you.

You fix your eyes on mine. You step toward me. I step toward you.

Yes! I hear you shout above the roar of the storm. And I hear your voice echo from the eastern horizon to the west.

Why have I not trusted you before? I wonder.

Walking toward you, across the uncertain surfaces is … the most natural, the most holy, the most joyful thing I can ever imagine doing.

I press against the wind. I run.

And I wish everyone could live this way. All of us, pressing forward, free, through the dark night, across the storm-tossed sea of our complex humanity.

Each of us, and all of us together, invited to something infinitely more than we have ever imagined.

This freedom, utter freedom in God, freedom in your Father's love, was the point of your living, your dying, and your rising from the dead.

This utter freedom in God, freedom in your Father's love, also is the point of my living, my dying, and my rising as well.

Amen.

EPILOGUE

HOW I PRAY ... AND
WHY I PRAY

I cannot write or speak of prayer apart from the one defining relationship that invites my prayer, and the way of life that demands it.

I mean relationship with Jesus, who is crucified Lord and risen Christ. A relationship I cannot fathom, and also the one relationship from which I cannot walk away.

And I mean the way of life which is the life of a disciple, a life lived as a servant of the Lord.

And I mean also the way of life which is the life of an apostle, a life lived as one who is sent by the Lord to stand in his place and to act on his behalf.

I am drawn to—indeed, sobered by—the intensity of the mission of apostle, sobered by the conditions of discipleship which Jesus spells out so clearly, especially in the Gospel of Matthew.

An opening Scripture: Matthew 10:34-39
Cutting to the heart of mission

> Whoever loves father or mother more than me is not worthy of
> me, ... and whoever does not take up his cross and follow after
> me is not worthy of me. Whoever finds his life will lose it, and
> whoever loses his life for my sake will find it.

Do not think that I have come to preach an easy message, you say,
Master, to your followers. *Do not think that I have come to approve your
comfortable way of life, unrocked by the urgency of the reign of God.*

These words of yours are hard to take, my Lord. You speak of
division, even within families. Son against father, daughter against
mother.

Do we not have enough division and strife already? Do not families
already suffer enough?

But the division of which you speak signals a deeper work, the hard
work where motives are purified, the hard work where mission is called
out and becomes inescapably clear.

The division of which you speak is the honest announcement that
we, who would be your followers, must either courageously step up or go
away.

You ask from us a quality of faith which is not a passive assent but
an active leaning in, an action, a consistent readiness to act, and to act
with the full authority of anointing in the Holy Spirit.

You insist that we determine clearly, decisively, who exactly we are
for, and focus fiercely on the details of the mission to which you
summon us.

Your words, my Lord, cut straight to the heart of me: "If you love father or mother more than me, you are not worthy of me," I hear you say. "If you do not adhere to the difficult path, you are not worthy of me."

You are not worthy of me.

These words burn to the core of my soul.

I know what I mean when I say: *Lord, I am not worthy of you.* I know myself too well to presume any merit of my own.

In fact, I find a certain consolation in openly saying to you: *Lord, I am not worthy of you.*

But when you, my Lord, you who know me through and through, you who know the subtle shades and undertones of my every motive, when you say to me: *You are not worthy of me,* then I am sobered.

You desire to claim, to occupy, the very center of me. More, you desire to actually and fully *be* the very center of me. You desire to permeate my being from the inner core to the outer edges, and beyond.

If you did not desire these things so passionately, your words would not sting so deeply.

An opening story: "I want to worship my Father"

It is the hour before dawn on Ash Wednesday morning. And as I begin Morning Prayer I feel caught up short, realizing that I have given no thought at all to how I will observe this Lenten season.

Giving up things seems so … spiritually futile. Whatever I give up would be in service to self-improvement. I can pursue self-improvement at some other time, maybe, but not in the season of Lent.

Perhaps I could try some new practices—more prayer, more outreach. Maybe I could make long-delayed amends with someone who has probably gotten over whatever the issue was and moved on.

Now, in the predawn silence, in the flickering light of the oil lamp before the sacred icon of Holy Trinity, I hear these words, interior and distinct: *I want to worship my Father in the temple of your life.*

As I picture this "temple" which is my life, and as I imagine Jesus worshiping his Father within this temple, I am stunned, utterly silenced, with the enormity of the invitation.

Instinctively I know that my Lent will not be about me "deciding" what I will give up, or what practices I will take on. My Lent will be about living the life which will allow the Lord to worship his Father from within the grit of my experience.

Suddenly I realize that the whole of my life becomes the temple. In fact, the whole of my life already is the temple. I have never before seen my life in this way. I am seeing it now.

I am sobered by this Lenten assignment, which also feels like an invitation. And which feels enormous, and ready to be life-changing.

In this predawn silence I discern with new urgency that how I live my life truly matters. How I pray matters. Not only to me, but to the Lord, who lives and prays to his Father through me.

How I pray

Church prays in many ways, through many forms of prayer. I do not pray them all.

Rather than feeling guilty, I feel focused.

Basically, I have seven ways of prayer. You may want to make your own list. You very well may have more ways of prayer than you realize. And you likely pray in some ways which I do not.

My seven ways of prayer include these:
1. Liturgical prayer and the Liturgy of the Hours
2. Modified lectio divina
3. Intercessions
4. One last prayer
5. My prayer on Fridays
6. Prayer in all those other places
7. A new form of examen

1. Liturgical prayer and the Liturgy of the Hours

All prayer, in some way, is the lifting of heart and mind to God.

Liturgical prayer, which surely expresses this lifting of heart and mind to God, is distinct for its underlying rhythm of the paschal cycle of dying and rising. Specifically, dying to self and receiving new life in Christ.

This lived experience of dying and rising, of dying and receiving new life in Christ, is the underlying vital rhythm of everything that lives, the underlying rhythm that pulses through all of creation.

Each of the sacraments—from sacraments of initiation and sustenance to sacraments of mission, to sacraments of spiritual and physical healing—each one expresses an individual's way of being faithful to God through the risen Lord.

In each sacramental experience, something of me is placed on the altar of sacrifice, invited to die, so that I can receive from that altar, which is Christ, new life in Christ.

Liturgical prayer gives me a way to be faithful to my humanity. The losses, the hopes, the times of testing, and the times of receiving unbidden blessings, everything that shapes my humanity—all of this is folded into the fabric of liturgical prayer.

The high point of my week is Sunday Eucharist, when I gather with my faith community to worship, to hear and ponder, to intercede, and to feast together at the divine banquet table.

Sunday Eucharist is the time when my big wicker basket is filled, I imagine, with warm fresh loaves which will nourish those whom I will encounter in the week ahead.

For the past forty-and-some years my interior life has rested upon the foundation of the particular form of liturgical prayer which is called the Liturgy of the Hours.

Growing from the ancient Jewish tradition of gathering for prayer at certain hours throughout the day, the Christian practice likewise "interrupts" the flow of the day with the praying of psalms and scripture readings.

This form of liturgical prayer is a way of lifting up as sacred the labors of the field, the lab, the classroom, the shop floor, the office, the home, the public spaces, the mundane and hidden places where worthy work gets done.

The psalms have endured through the ages as poignant expressions of what is most urgent, and hopeful, most anguished and trusting and true, within the human experience. They express the soul's radical dependence on the protection and mercy of God.

The psalms in the Liturgy of the Hours offer me a rhythm of prayer which shapes the trajectory of my week. They move me through the hard work of human experience, pleading for divine mercy, and rejoicing in God's compassion and nearness.

They shape my recalling the Lord's passion and death, and his undying trust in his Fathers protection.

The psalms carry me toward Sunday Eucharist, and shape the Christian community's celebration of the risen Christ.

For me, Morning Prayer from the Liturgy of the Hours has become the indispensable prayer.

And I mean unrushed Morning Prayer, especially unrushed on my busy days, and especially when my travel schedule requires me to leave my home at three-thirty for an early morning flight.

On these travel days I rise before midnight, in order to hold open a space for additional unrushed prayer. I cannot explain the joy and freedom from fatigue which I experience upon arising. Nor can I explain the energy I feel at the end of these days, refreshed as though I had had a full night's sleep.

In holding open a generous space for unrushed Morning Prayer, I hold open a space for the soul, uncomplicated by schedules and assignments that soon enough will demand my attention.

In praying the psalms of Morning Prayer, I enter into the eternal and wordless, loving conversation of Holy Trinity. I awaken inside *kairos* time, or "time outside of time," before I step into the measured, limited space of *kronos* time.

When I pray the psalms in the Liturgy of the Hours, I pray on behalf of the world.

If the psalms of anguish do not really capture where I am "at" right now, I pray them anyway, faithfully. Because right now, far too much of humanity, and far too much of creation, is in anguish.

And knowingly or not, humanity in its anguish, all of creation in its anguish, is counting on the faithful ones to plead the cause of justice and restoration and mercy before the throne of God.

Just as Jesus interceded for all of humanity, so I must intercede for all of humanity, in his name, in my time. In doing so, I discover that the boundaries dissolve between my soul and the soul of the world.

2. Modified lectio divina: Praying the Gospels in a new way

I have experienced the formal process of *lectio divina,* the time-honored five-step process of meditatively praying a passage of Scripture.

But sometimes I forget the five steps. Or I worry that I might get them in the wrong order. Or leave one out. There are so many.

The five steps, which I will name in familiar English rather than in the customary Latin, are these:

Step 1: Lection, or reading what is written on the page; simply reading the story, the narrative, the teaching, whatever is presented.

Step 2: Meditation, or sitting with what I have read in light of my own life and circumstances.

Step 3: Prayer, or offering a grateful response to my encounter with the Word.

Step 4: Contemplation, or going deeper with the text in order to experience conversion through this encounter.

Step 5: Action, or actually living differently, more compassionately, more honestly, more generously, more justly, as a fruit of this deeper encounter with the Word.

I simply enter into the reading and let the reading carry me to what I need to notice and experience.

And what I have discovered is that the more fully I enter into the Word, the more fully the Word enters into me.

With the Gospels, I have come to pray the reading in a more intimate way. I actually read the story aloud to the Lord, recounting to him this conversation with his disciples, this particular encounter with his adversaries, this healing of the sick.

In other words, I change the narrative from third person to second person, sharing with Jesus these scenes from his life.

For example, in chapter four of the Gospel of Luke, Jesus has just delivered his inaugural teaching on the passage from Isaiah. The passage reads:

> They rose up and expelled him from the town, leading him to the brow of the hill on which it was built and intending to hurl him over the edge. But he went straight through their midst and walked away.

I might read the passage this way:

> They rose up, my Lord, and expelled you from the town, leading you to the brow of the hill on which it was built and intending to hurl you over the edge. But you went straight through their midst and walked away.

In shifting from distant third person to a more intimate second person, I enter conversationally into the story. I enter as a disciple, into a direct and living encounter with the Master, in order to accompany him on his journey to Jerusalem.

And in his arrest and trial and crucifixion, this more intimate reading of the narrative draws me into more earnest apprenticeship with the Lord. As he undergoes the ultimate test of faithfulness to his mission, he shows me how, in my time of testing, I must be faithful to my own.

3. Intercessions

At the close of Morning Prayer, somewhere in the hour of dawn or early daylight, or in winter when the Big Dipper arcs across the predawn sky, I step out into my yard to pray my intercessions.

Praying outdoors feels expansive, walking, as I do, outside the walls of my living quarters.

Intercession is a form of prayer in which I "stand in the gap" and ask God's protection, God's anointing, God's favor, on the life of another, or on particular circumstances.

I do not pray for everyone, nor for every situation. But I notice who has been entrusted to my care, and I notice, too, what situations weigh upon my heart. And these I lift up in prayer.

First, I lift up Pope Francis, who lives openly, prophetically, and therefore precariously on the world stage. I pray an anointing, a deep fragrant soaking in the Holy Spirit, in every area of his life and work this day.

Next I lift up the world, in all of its beauty and urgency of life, in all of its birthing and dying, its waxing and waning. I also lift up the world in all of its anguish, the suffering of human flesh and human spirit, and the suffering of creation, through all forms of oppression through greed and injustice.

Equally, I lift up all those who enter courageously and at great cost into the dangerous places to physically relieve suffering and to restore the dignity, the humanity, of those who suffer.

And I lift up all those who often risk their lives to advocate for the cause of justice and equity and right. On them I pray a soaking of the Holy Spirit in their endeavors today.

When I pray for the world, recent news reports and stories of courageous acts come to mind, as well as local actions and initiatives in the cause of compassion and justice.

Next, I lift up those entrusted to me. I pray for family members, each by name. I recall each one's gifts, and challenges, and opportunities to touch lives. I pray a soaking of the Holy Spirit upon each one in all of their endeavors this day.

I lift up a few others whom I know, who do some very heavy lifting in the work of bringing about the reign of God. With each one, I pray a deep anointing, a soaking in the Holy Spirit, in their labors and in their lives this day.

And finally, I lift up "your servant, Mary Sharon." I look upon her with the same generous love and compassion with which I look upon these others, in a way I could not do if I were praying for "me."

I lift up her labors, her hopes, her openness to invitations to be used in service to the Lord. And I pray a deep and fragrant anointing, a deep soaking in the Holy Spirit, in every area of her life and work.

I pray these prayers, I bless God, and then I let them go.

At noon I do what I oftentimes would rather not do: I interrupt my work in order to enter again, this time briefly, into my prayer space, again in intercession.

I revisit the day's Gospel reading, and find a passage which I can chew and savor briefly.

And then I lift up each of those, by name, whom I accompany in spiritual direction. Lovingly, mindful of their lives and struggles and hopes, I invoke the deep and fragrant anointing of the Holy Spirit upon their lives this day.

4. One last prayer

The anguish of the world and the precarity of human life does not escape my notice. So at night I enter one last time into my prayer space, to pray one last prayer, before I go to bed.

Briefly I pray to the Lord "for all those who will die this night and in the coming day, especially those whose lives and circumstances are known to you alone."

I pray for those who will die "frail and in the shadows." I pray for those who will die "alone, or feeling abandoned."

I entrust them all to the great compassion of God. And I know that this prayer is sufficient. In this last brief moment in the day I put my heart, one more time, with the heart of God.

Prayer of intercession teaches me to pay attention to what breaks my heart. Because, I believe, what breaks my heart first breaks the heart of God.

5. My prayer on Fridays

This practice of one last prayer "for those who will die this night and in the coming day" has led me to a further practice: praying the Office for the Dead on Fridays.

The psalms and readings for Morning Prayer and Evening Prayer in the Office for the Dead are tender, compassionate, full of pleading, and full of assurance of God's mercy.

I can best describe this Friday practice as putting my heart with the heart of humanity, and also with the heart of the Lord, on the day which commemorates his passion, death, and burial.

The blood of humanity flows in my veins, I discover. The blood of humanity flowed in Jesus' veins, too.

The breath that flows and the heartbeat that pulses through humanity also flows and pulses through me. It is the same breath, the same heartbeat, that flowed and pulsed through the Lord.

In fact, what I discern is that in this world there is only one heartbeat. There is only one breath, originating in God and giving life to all that is, the breath of the Holy Spirit.

Praying the Office for the Dead on Friday moves me directly toward Eucharist on Sunday, and especially toward that moment in the preparation of the gifts when the wine is decanted into the waiting cups.

Wine poured out, blood of humanity, especially in the lives of those who have died in the preceding week. The labors, the anguish, the hopes, the lives poured out in service. Some lives poured out in tragedy. Some poured out in vain.

Yet all poured out as the imperfect yet now perfected offering to God, in Christ.

6. Prayer in all those other places

Call it another form of *lectio divina*. Call it "spontaneous" or "enfleshed" intercession. Call it meditation in motion.

But a certain form of prayer comes over me when I am in all those other places, among "my people"—my downtown people—people who are just like me, and people who are not just like me.

I discover that my encounters with my people also are encounters with my God.

My motive for being downtown among my people is love.

And so this form of prayer—yes, I will call it enfleshed intercession —is an expression of love, a way I strive to express a more attentive, loving, compassionate way of being in the world of real people with painful stories from checkered pasts, who carry unexplainable hope held together with gossamer.

When I look into the eyes of Chuck, with that real zipper of a scar running the length of his long, sad face, and listen to his story; when I sit beside Treetop at Novella Cafe and share a sandwich with him and his lady friend; when I come across Gonzalo in his wheelchair on one street corner or another, and bend down and give him a hug; when I weep with Carla, the young mom in the Greyhound station who is traveling to see her little boy—in all of these moments I discover that I am doing a living form of *lectio divina.*

I am reading the Word fresh off the page of my experience in this moment. I touch the flesh of Jesus, cleverly disguised as Chuck, or Treetop, or Gonzalo, or Carla. I intercede for the ones at the margins, those same margins where Jesus can be found.

My prayer in all these other places may or may not have words. It is the steady compassionate glance, the intentional encounter, the hug which I know will impress upon my clothing the tired smell of the poor.

7. A new form of examen

At day's end I have never felt drawn toward the scrutinizing work of examination of conscience. I deal with transgressions when they come up. And by the end of the day I am not really wanting to revisit what is now past.

I would rather look into the eye of judgment as I gaze upon the face of Christ, than ponder a list of ways I did not measure up today.

So I have begun, in the evenings, to sit with the questions I pose at the end of Part 2, five questions to deepen the conversation of prayer.

I reword the questions here to place them within the context of an evening examen. I invite you to let these questions minister to you.

Question 1: Today, what gave me joy?

Was it my joy? Was it someone else's joy in which I shared?

How did I bless God by entering into the experience?

Conversely, did I rush past the experience, not wanting to slow down? Did I regard it as nothing?

Question 2: Today, what robbed me of joy?

Was it an undesired turn of events affecting me personally? Was it an interior disposition, an attitude, a hardness of heart, a mean spirit within me?

What might God be showing me in this unexpected turn of events?

Conversely, did I ride roughshod over the experience, adding a new layer of callous to my spirit?

Question 3: Today, what broke my heart?

Was it an encounter with someone's suffering? Was it seeing goodness or hope or tender love crushed? Was it unexpected loss, whether mine or another's?

Am I able to put my broken heart with the broken heart of God?

Conversely, did I "scan and scroll" through the experience, and perhaps decide: "I'm OK with that"?

Question 4: Today, what was I resisting?

Was it an invitation to conversion of heart? An invitation to live more simply, or more generously? An invitation to step beyond my excuses and to finally take action? An invitation to acknowledge and bless others whom I have dismissed in the past?

Am I willing to sit with God, revisit the invitation, and act differently now?

Conversely, am I determined to not be moved by the invitations that I wish would just go away?

Question 5: Today, what did I finally accept?

Was it the unconditional love of a friend, a family member, a caregiver, a stranger? Did I finally accept genuine forgiveness and restoration of lost friendship with another, or with God? Did I finally accept the reality of an irreversible loss? Or the answer I did not want to a prayer I have held dear?

Am I able to breathe deeply into this new reality which holds the power to open me to my fuller self-in-God?

Conversely, do I still insist, despite the evidence, that I will have it my way or not at all?

Why I pray

I ask myself: Could I just not pray?

Could I imagine myself saying: "I have prayed enough in this lifetime; now it is someone else's turn."

Or, "Enough of early rising. I think I shall start to sleep in."

Honestly, I cannot imagine these things. I cannot imagine not praying.

So I have to ask myself: Why, then, do I pray? Why do I actually pray? What impels me?

Three answers emerge.

First, I pray because I am *invited* to pray.

Just as I was invited into being. I was invited into the homely life of these particular parents, and this particular family.

Just as I was invited into Christian community. My parents brought me early to baptism. But it was the Lord who did the inviting.

Had I sought baptism as an adult, my initiative still would have been only a response to the Lord's gracious invitation.

Therefore, I am *invited* into life in Christ Jesus. I am *invited* to remain with him, and to reveal him everywhere. To reveal him joyfully, generously, motivated by love which is the wellspring of gratitude.

Always I am invited to something more, to astonishing great good, beyond what I could imagine.

In prayer, I am invited to enter into Jesus, who is crucified Lord and risen Christ. Invited to enter in so completely that I become lost in him. Living no longer for myself but gladly for him who for my sake died and was raised, as Saint Paul writes.

I am invited to enter into Christ Jesus, so that I might live, no longer I, but that he might live in me.

Second, I pray because I have been *anointed* to pray in the place of Jesus in my twenty-first century world.

This is no small anointing. And therefore this praying in the place of Jesus is no small prayer.

I have been anointed in the Spirit of the risen Lord. I find this astonishing.

"As the Father has sent me," Jesus tells those early apostles on the day of his resurrection, "so I send you."

And then he breathes on them and says, "Receive the Holy Spirit."

I cannot ignore the direct parallel. For I too have been anointed to be an apostle of the risen Lord. "As the Father has sent me, exactly so, in the same manner," Jesus says, "do I send you."

This "you" is personal. The risen Lord is speaking to me.

Jesus, sent by his Father, is the first apostle, we could say, the Protoapostle.

Yet he is the first of many who also are sent to reveal, as he revealed, the reign of God, each in our own time. He showed us how it is done, this work of being an apostle, being sent on mission in service to his Father's willing, the reign of God.

This anointing carries an urgency. All I need to do is to look around me, or listen to the daily news, to sense the urgency of my mission.

Not to rescue everyone and remedy all ills and address all injustices. But to live, unafraid and unashamed, in the power of my anointing for the good of the world which I touch.

To actually notice what is broken, to be moved to action by what is hurting, and to hold open a space for grace to appear. And to work as I am able to reveal the reign of God in my place and time, according to the ways I have been gifted.

To pray in the place of Jesus in my twenty-first century world means to yearn, here and now, for what Jesus yearns for, in this time and place.

In order to pray well I have to pay close attention to what breaks the heart of God. I have to weep for the things that make God weep. This, too, is prayer.

And third, I pray because Jesus is not yet finished praying to his Father.

Jesus is not finished worshiping his Father, yes. And he is not yet finished interceding. Because his heart of flesh continues to feel the wounds of the world, and also, to feel the world's hope.

Yet he feels the wounds and the hopes of the world, and intercedes, through this particular heart of flesh, my heart.

And he intercedes through yours. My tears and yours are his tears. My sighs and your sighs are the sighs of his Holy Spirit within us.

As long as there is human anguish and human hope, Jesus, who is crucified Lord and risen Christ, will continue to pray through you, through me.

ABOUT THE AUTHOR

Mary Sharon Moore is a Catholic writer, speaker, teacher, and spiritual director, whose work is dedicated to awakening men and women of Christian faith to the power of their sacramental anointing. Her evangelizing ministry spans the United States.

Mary Sharon believes that every baptized person has been anointed to stand in the place of the risen Lord in the world they touch. She also believes that the world itself is waiting for men and women of Christian faith to wake up to the power of their anointing, and to reveal in fresh and powerful ways the reign of God in our time.

Other books by Mary Sharon Moore include:
Anointed for a Purpose: Confirmed for life in the 21st century (2012)
> (also available as a 4-CD audiobook on the Store page at marysharonmoore.com)

Conformed to Christ: Discoveries in the maturing Christ-centered life (2016)
Living in God's Economy: A "domestic church" resource for Gospel living (2016)
Moving in God's Direction: Essentials of Christ-centered spiritual and vocational direction (2012)
Seven Last Words and Eight Words of Easter: Meditations for your journey to Pentecost (2013)
Touching the Reign of God: Bringing theological reflection to daily life (2009)

These books, plus a catalog of Mary Sharon's parish missions, retreats, and workshops, can be found at marysharonmoore.com.

MARY SHARON MOORE | marysharonmoore.com
Eugene, Oregon | 541.687.2046 | marysharonmoore@gmail.com
Honest talk on the nature of God's calling in our time

Made in the USA
San Bernardino, CA
10 December 2017